Into Their Hands
at any cost

ISBN: 978-1-936208-00-5

Layout and cover design: Lydia Zook
Front cover photos: © iStockphoto

Printed in the USA
Second printing: December 2010

For more information about Christian Aid Ministries, see page 183

Published by:
TGS International
P.O. Box 355
Berlin, Ohio 44610 USA
Phone: 330·893·4828
Fax: 330·893·2305

Harvey Yoder

Into Their Hands
at any cost

Introduction

Although no one knows exactly when the first Bibles were smuggled into communist countries, we do know that in the 1960s there was already concern among Western churches for believers in communist Eastern Europe. As news leaked out about the difficult conditions and desperate times behind the Iron Curtain, people's hearts began to feel for their brethren in distress. One of the greatest burdens the West faced was how to get the printed Word to their suffering brothers.

Bibles were printed in Western countries by the thousands, organizations mobilized volunteers, and the great migration of Bibles began. But this book is not the story of how the Bibles were printed. This is a small glimpse of how some of those Bibles reached their final destinations. Eternity alone will reveal how many Bibles streamed across the borders and into the hands of the desperately hungry. We know that thousands, perhaps millions, of Bibles were transported hundreds of miles into the oppressed countries. Some Soviet-bloc countries were much more open, and people could easily, if not openly, get their own Bibles. For others, it was costly not only in monetary value, but in danger of prison and sometimes death.

Perhaps many of us have read or heard stories of brave smugglers who were imprisoned, tortured, and even martyred for their work in getting Bibles to the population. Truly, many suffered bravely for their God-given vision, but this book is not necessarily about those people. This is a collection of stories about ordinary people involved in God's work. Ordinary, in that their deeds may not have seemed great and noble, yet they were extraordinary by simple virtue of their willingness to answer the call. They were willing to face the risks and hardships and still get their job done.

The stories are arranged to show the movement of Bibles from Western Europe into communist Eastern Europe. The first chapters relate to Bibles crossing the border into Romania. The next chapters are about the distribution of Bibles in Romania as well as the movement of Russian Bibles through Romania en route to the Soviet Union. The last chapters track the journey of these Russian Bibles into the Soviet Union and finally into the hands of Russian believers.

So, we present these stories to you. Some names and cities have been changed by request, others have not; it doesn't really matter, for they all worked for God's glory. All of the stories actually happened. I have used a writer's liberty in filling in details and adding local flavor in order to write this book. If there are mistakes, omissions, or other inaccuracies, I take responsibility for them all.

It is our desire that God will use these testimonies to further our walk with Him, to deepen our appreciation for the brave men and women who opened their lives to be used by God in His work, and to better understand how Bibles got into countries behind the Iron Curtain.

—*Harvey Yoder*

Contents

Chapter One

How Did I Ever Get Into This?

From her seat on the mattress in the back of the Volkswagen minibus, Irene could enjoy the relatively flat terrain of the Hungarian countryside. It was late summer, and here and there a few trees showed early splashes of color, although there was none of the brilliant foliage she pictured on the maple trees back home in her parents' yard in Pennsylvania. Here, autumn seemed to come quietly and gently with more subdued, muted colors.

But it was warm—almost hot. She wiped her forehead and peered forward through the windshield. For a moment she watched the straight road stretching ahead of them and then glanced at the two boys sitting up front. George was driving and Rick sat silently in the passenger's seat.

Irene checked her watch. "I think we must be close to the border," she called above the noise of the motor.

George glanced at her in the rearview mirror. "Yes, it's not far at all. Are you ready?"

"Yes. I mean, I guess I am. How ready can you be?"

"That's the question. How ready can you be?" George chuckled. "Rick, are you ready?"

"No," Rick replied quietly. "But I know God is."

Shifting slightly on the mattress, Irene was sure she could

feel the tops of the cardboard boxes lining the floor of the van beneath her. There were no seats in the back, just this mattress strategically covering the boxes.

Their camping gear was stashed all the way at the back of the vehicle. A camp stove to make meals, boxes of food, and several large containers of water testified to the nature of their trip. Or did they? Irene looked critically at them. Was the ruse convincing enough? They had actually used the camping gear. More than once they had pulled off to the side of the road, and she had made meals for the three of them.

"Are you still suffering from those doughy pancakes?" Irene directed the question forward.

George grimaced and bent over, clutching his stomach with his free hand. But the twinkle in his eye as he looked back at Irene showed that he was not holding any grudges.

"They weren't really all that bad," Rick replied encouragingly as he turned to look at the girl on the mattress.

"Well, I admit they were doughy," Irene chuckled. "I thought the frying pan was hot enough, but when I put the batter in, it hardly even sizzled."

"The extra weight in the middle of my stomach will help keep my feet on the ground up ahead," George said, nodding at the border control between Hungary and Romania.

Irene saw the cluster of buildings rising from the horizon. "Lord, please," was all she could say.

Crossing from Austria into Hungary had been fairly smooth, but they had not been in Hungary very long before Irene began seeing evidence of the repressive communist regime. However, she had been told that the crossing into Romania would be the real test.

"Did I do okay at the last border crossing?" Irene inquired anxiously as the van slowed to join the queue of vehicles waiting to cross into Romania.

"You did well," Rick assured her. "Actually, I was trying too hard to act normal to really watch what you were doing."

"Remember your orientation," George reminded her. "We are a group of campers going into Romania as tourists."

The van inched forward as the line ahead of them moved.

"Anyone want a drink?" Irene poured some water from the canteen as she reflected. The boys were warm and thirsty and reached eagerly for the water Irene handed forward.

Bibles. Yes, they really were trying to smuggle Bibles into a communist country. Not just any Bibles, but Russian Bibles, destined for the Soviet Union itself. Irene had no idea how these Bibles would be taken across the border into the Soviet Union once they got them into Romania—assuming they got them safely there. She knew the boys had an address for someone in the city of *Iaşi** where they were to deliver the Bibles. This was their part in the journey of many steps to get God's Word into the hands of Christians in the Soviet Union.

"Get your passports ready," George reminded them. Two cars ahead of them, the gate was opening for the next group of vehicles.

They passed through the gate, and an officer waved them to the side.

"What do we do here?" Irene wanted to know.

"We have to get our Romanian visas," George replied briefly.

Irene climbed out the side door of the van. As the door slammed shut, she looked once more at the brown boxes un-

Refer to glossary on pages 185-186 for pronunciations or definitions of italicized words.

der the mattress. They all looked the same from the outside, but Irene remembered how carefully she had helped to pack them back in Stuttgart, Germany. Fourteen boxes had been placed side by side on the floor of the van. Three of them were packed with used clothing, and those three had been put directly inside the passenger side door. If the border police wanted to check their cargo, hopefully they would open the clothing boxes.

Trying to appear nonchalant, Irene joined George and Rick in the line leading to the visa kiosk. Progress was slow as the officials took their time, studying the passports intently and barking questions. Irene did not understand the language, yet she could understand the no-nonsense tone of their voices. A tingle of apprehension ran up her spine.

"You'll need to fill out these forms," George told Irene as he handed her the documents. He had crossed the border numerous times and was very familiar with the procedure. Irene was glad for his confidence, because she felt as out of place as a Pennsylvania farm girl could.

"Here it asks for your name," George explained helpfully. "Your passport number goes here. This is place of birth. Write your nationality here. Date of birth here. And there, reason for requesting visa. You're a tourist, remember?"

Irene wished she felt more like a tourist. How did tourists act? Probably they would be curious, she decided. So after the forms were completed, she carefully observed her surroundings.

It was evident they were in a tightly controlled area. Not only was the gate behind them closed, there was also a barrier ahead of them. Just beyond that, she could see another barrier. Low, gray metal buildings with barred windows lined the passageways where vehicles either inched forward or were pulled aside. There was really not very much activity. Most of the drivers and passengers were seated inside their vehicles, waiting.

She wanted to ask George what they were waiting for but thought it might be better if she didn't speak. The atmosphere was almost eerie and, yes, definitely repressive. At each gate and barrier, uniformed guards stood stiffly in their drab uniforms.

"We could easily be here for several hours." George's quiet voice broke into her reverie. "My longest wait at this particular border was almost twenty-three hours."

Irene gasped. "A whole day?"

George smiled at her and raised his eyebrows. He nodded.

Rick said nothing.

"Tell me, Irene, where were you born?" George asked.

Before answering, Irene glanced cautiously at the kiosk. There was no one there!

"He left," she said in bewilderment.

Rick nodded placidly. "That happens."

"But … ?" Irene felt impatient. Surely there was a better system for running a border control than this! She looked at the long line of vehicles waiting to enter the border zone. Glancing at her watch, she realized they had already been at the border for forty-five minutes!

"Hey, where were you born?" George persisted.

Heads swiveled as people turned to look at them.

"Oh, uh, in Pennsylvania," Irene answered and then asked quietly, "Should we be talking?"

George laughed. "We are just being Westerners. People from the West aren't used to being quiet. Especially Americans. Besides, everyone already knows where we are from."

"But how?" Irene wanted to know. "We don't really look that different."

"They just know," George replied. "If you rarely see foreigners and suddenly one appears, you just know. It's mostly mannerisms that give it away."

"Then we're marked."

"Well, there are quite a number of international students coming into these countries right now. Groups of young people traveling together are not unusual at all."

Irene nodded. She knew that was how this particular Bible smuggling route had started. When two very successful Bible smugglers had been blacklisted and were no longer able to cross into the Soviet-controlled countries, the idea of using traveling students had been birthed.

Recruited from all over the free world, these groups of young people joined the hosts of college and university students who were hiking through the woodlands and forests of Romania, Poland, and other Soviet-bloc countries. The Bible smuggling bands tried to blend in by joining the holiday backpackers.

Irene glanced around her again. She could see no other student groups. They had probably returned to school already.

Ah! The officer was back. Or was it another officer? Irene wasn't sure. They all looked alike in their uniforms.

When she pushed her passport and application form under the steel bars, Irene tried to still her rapidly beating heart. The barrage of questions directed at her had no meaning. She shrugged her shoulders and said helplessly, "I'm sorry, I don't speak your language. I speak English."

She remembered how someone had instructed her. "Don't offer any information that you are not specifically asked."

Well, she couldn't really offer anything now for she did not even know what he asked.

The officer grumbled under his breath and barked into a two-way radio. There was a crackle, and a voice seemed to answer through the static, but Irene doubted she would understand the voice even if it had been in English.

The officer gave an explosive retort. Then he turned to the youth and asked more questions. Irene tried her best to smile, but she wasn't sure how successful she was. It might have looked more like a grimace, but she just shook her head.

George, too, shrugged his shoulders and said, "We speak English. We are tourists. We want to explore your country and see your cities."

This lengthy answer apparently irritated the officer. Once more he pushed a button and spoke loudly into the radio. This time there was no answer. Grabbing their passports, he flipped pages and began stamping. Shoving them back at the three, he indicated they were to leave.

"Did we get the visas?" Irene asked as they headed back to the van.

"Yes. He was frustrated that there was no interpreter available," George chuckled. "I guess they thought the students wouldn't be coming through here for awhile."

"So you …" Irene began. Her voice trailed off as George frowned slightly at her.

Oh, yes. No questions. Well, at least none about knowing languages.

"Don't even let anyone know that you know a dialect of German," she had been told. "It is better for you to always speak English."

Not everything made sense to her, but she remembered that her parents used to tell her when she was an inquisitive child, "If you observe closely, many of your questions will be answered eventually."

Irene couldn't help but ask when they were back at the van, "What now? Can we go?"

"Someone will come and inspect our van," Rick told her.

That someone was coming right then. Irene watched as he told George to open the back.

There was the camp stove, streaked with smoke. The cooking utensils, the coffee pot, and the box with their food were all inspected. Then the inspector went to the side door.

One part of Irene did not want to watch, yet she could not keep her eyes away as the inspector reached for the boxes under the mattress. Oh, no, was that a box of Bibles? Would they be turned back? Would the inspector get angry at them for trying to take Bibles into Romania? Could he read Russian and know they were destined for the Soviet Union? Like startled sparrows, Irene's thoughts dashed through her mind.

The inspector tugged the top of the box open, revealing nothing but clothes inside! Irene almost gasped. She was certain they had put Bibles into that box. What was happening?

He skipped the next box and reached for the third in line. By this time her head was spinning. If the first was clothes, and she had thought that one had Bibles, then what was in this one? It would have to have Bibles, right?

No Bibles. Just more clothing. A woman's white sweater lay neatly folded on top of the pile of clothes. The inspector lifted the sweater and peered down the side. Nothing but clothes. He mumbled something under his breath and reached for a box that was only partially visible. He had to lift the mattress up and pull the box out so he could open it.

"Clothes," Irene kept whispering to herself. "Clothes."

There were only three boxes of clothes. Would he check any of the other boxes? Would God turn Bibles into clothes for the border crossing? She knew it would be no more difficult than turning water into wine.

When the third box revealed yet more clothes, the inspector turned with an exasperated look to the three as if to ask, "Why so many clothes?"

"Well, you know, sir, how women are." George answered his look with a wave in Irene's direction. "They want a set of clothes for traveling, and later something might spill on them while cooking, and then for the evening, why, who knows what will happen so that another set is needed. Multiply this by two weeks or so to see that a lot of clothes are needed."

Irene was too flabbergasted to say anything. She stared at George with her mouth opening and closing. Why, he knew those weren't her clothes! Besides …

George waggled his eyebrows at the indignant girl, and when the inspector stamped a paper and handed it to George, she almost had to laugh. Of course, the inspector hadn't understood George's tirade. He had done it to get a reaction from her.

Rick gave her an understanding smile, but George was saying, "Get in!"

Irene clambered back onto the mattress and looked with glee at the last gate that swung open to let them through. They had passed! Praise God, they were headed into Romania—with the Bibles!

"God," she breathed softly. "I still don't know how it happened that he just chose the boxes with clothes. Ah, it didn't just happen. You guided his hand to the boxes you wanted him to inspect."

A feeling of awe swept over her. To see such an obvious sign of God's blessing on their work gave her faith an enormous boost. Yes, this was God's work.

.   .   .   .   .

"I thought once we were inside Romania there would be no more police controls or checkpoints," Irene told the boys. "But there are so many! Outside every major city, at the center of the villages … they are all over!"

"And now we need to buy gas. Or benzene, as they call it here." George frowned at the gas gauge.

"Almost at Iaşi," Rick told the other two, looking at the map. Their trip had taken them from the western edge of Romania, across the mountainous region of the Carpathians, and now through the rolling countryside as they headed east.

"Another checkpoint," George groaned as they slowed down and began to creep toward the guard tower. Two policemen standing beside the road were monitoring all the traffic.

George knew the proper protocol. Go very slowly, and if an officer raised his white club, you were to pull over.

"Bet I could outrace any of those puny-looking police 'cruisers,' " George mumbled. "But they do have two-way radios, so I know that wouldn't work."

Once again, Irene was acutely aware of the boxes of Bibles under the mattress. God had protected them so far. Would they be able to get to their destination without being discovered?

"Don't look at the officers," George advised. "I'll pretend I don't know what they want."

It didn't work. The officer stepped out onto the road, stretching his white stick toward them as their van approached the painted line in front of them.

"Good day," George said cheerfully as he rolled his window down and addressed the officer. "How are you this fine day? You know you have a beautiful country here. We've enjoyed the scenery along the way."

Meanwhile, the officer was holding out his hand and trying to say something. "No English," he said finally and repeated a string of words.

"No Romanian," George said cheerfully, shrugging his shoulders and completely ignoring the obvious intent of the officer asking for their documents.

"No Romanian," George repeated as he leaned forward, jabbing his finger at the gas gauge. "No benzene, either! Can you tell me where to buy benzene?" George pointed repeatedly at the gauge every time the officer asked a question.

When a second officer approached them, there was a discourse between the two. Suddenly the first officer pointed to himself and then to the gauge, indicating he would accompany them to buy gas!

"No, no. No need. Just draw map." George was no longer quite his chatty self. "Where? How far?" He waved his hand toward the city.

But the officer insisted. He even laughed as he tried to communicate with these "tourists."

Irene thought of the irony of it all. One of the people they wanted to avoid the most was sitting inside the van with them.

It was at times like this when it seemed almost impossible to continue believing that they could ever be successful in carrying out their mission.

Thankfully, the distance to the gas station was not far. The officer was very helpful and the service station attendant was soon filling their tank. George thanked the policeman and tried to shake his hand in farewell. The policeman ignored the proffered handshake and made efforts to climb back into the van. He had obviously enjoyed his outing and even indicated with signs that he would ride with them further!

"We go that way," George said, pointing at random down the road and hoping that was not the way the officer wanted to go. To his chagrin, the officer nodded happily.

"Wait!" George pulled on his sleeve. "I want to have my picture taken with you. Here, you come out with me. Irene, you come and pose with us while Rick takes our picture."

As soon as the camera was pulled out of the case and the policeman realized what George was trying to tell him, his face grew very concerned.

"No!" He used one of the few English words he knew. Then he pantomimed what would happen and slapped imaginary handcuffs onto George's wrists.

"Oh, sorry. No pictures? I apologize." George put the camera away.

But the ruse worked. The officer backed off, and without shaking hands or telling them goodbye, he went inside the gas station.

"Whew! I wonder how often he has ridden in a van full of Bibles before!" Rick said as he smoothed his hair. "I was praying and praying all the while and wondering how God was going to get us out of that situation."

"Yeah, me too," George said. It was obvious the experience had been a definite strain on his nerves. "It delivered us from having our van inspected at the checkpoint, but I was expecting anytime that our friend would suddenly wonder what was under our mattress."

"I marvel at how the Lord continues to protect us," Irene said softly. "It seems as though an angel host is surrounding us and taking us through each situation. At least so far," she added soberly, thinking of the unknown ahead of them.

"My grace is sufficient for thee," Rick quoted. "I really want to take that promise for each moment. My trust in the mighty power of God is growing."

The other two nodded.

. . . . .

"Take a deep breath," Irene told herself, fanning her hot, sweating face with the paperback book she had brought along. "They will be back soon. 'My grace is sufficient for thee.' How I need that for right now." The city moved around her with nothing remotely familiar to her. Everything was strange.

That she and their van were strange was quite evident too. It had been evident for the last four hours as she sat inside the hot vehicle, waiting. Where were George and Rick? She checked her watch yet again. One o'clock.

Two adolescent boys slowed down on the sidewalk and gaped at her open-mouthed. As they walked slowly past the parked Volkswagen, their heads kept turning more and more while their bodies pulled them on down the street.

"Like the chickens at home on the farm," Irene muttered, laughing a little. She had often been fascinated by the hens, how that, as she lifted them from the nesting boxes, she could move their bodies back and forth and yet their heads would stay in the same place. Sighing, she looked up the street to where the boys had disappeared. Still no sign of her comrades.

She wanted to get out of the van to see better because the high rise apartment buildings blocked her view, but she felt unsure about leaving the security of the van.

"I have no idea where to go," George had said after they arrived in Iaşi that morning. "Here is the address, but how can I find it if there are no street signs?"

"I'll bet that is what they want," Irene said. "They don't want foreigners to find their way around the city."

Rick nodded. "I think you're right." At first they had driven around hoping to stumble across some familiar sign. Although the traffic was not as heavy as it was in American cities, it was no more patient. Horns blared as irate drivers pulled out and zoomed around the bumbling van with French license plates. Once, a man had leaned out as he was passing and yelled a string of words at them.

"Time like this, it's good not to know Romanian," George quipped.

Then they had found this spot, and the boys went on foot, hunting for the address where they had been told to leave the Bibles.

Irene had been fascinated, for the first hour at least, by the strangeness of a Romanian city. The people going about their business, the children passing by, even the curious and hungry dogs inspecting everything had at first been quite entertaining. Nothing at all like Pennsylvania, she thought. Or like the little village of Villy Montinique in France.

It was almost like a dream that she was here, inside a communist country. A year ago, if someone had told her she would be involved in Bible smuggling, she would surely have laughed in disbelief.

It had all started when Brother David had spoken at their church back home. She had been all ears as he spoke of the condition of the believers in the Soviet Union and in the other Soviet-bloc countries. "They need Bibles. The need is so great, yet we are not doing enough to get the Word of God into their hands."

Irene had felt a sudden lurching inside her. She wanted to help!

Yet, as David continued to talk, she found out that he had already gotten the quota of young people he needed for the trip that summer. He had explained how the new way of sending "camping" youth into the countries was proving successful.

Afterwards she had met David. "I would be interested in going, but I understand you already have your people all lined up."

At first David had said nothing, but just stared intently at her. What was he looking at? She wondered if he saw something strange about her.

"I do need you," he had suddenly said as though he had come to a conclusion, "but not to take Bibles. I need you to help Sofia."

Sofia, he explained, was the wife of the mission director in France, and she needed help. She had four little boys and crowds of people going through their house; there was a desperate need for some assistance. "I see you can work, and that will be a direct link in the chain of taking Bibles effectively into the countries."

With bewildering speed, Irene had found herself traveling to Philadelphia to get her visa, and because her airline ticket was bought on the spur of the moment, she ended up traveling to France by herself.

"Whew," Irene said to herself now, and not because of the heat inside the van. "That was quite the trip."

Inexperienced and naïve to the ways of travel, she had been incredibly relieved when she had finally arrived at her destination.

"I have to go to town," Sofia had said the first thing the next morning. "You may wash the dishes."

Well, four boys, a husband, and who knows how many visitors must have used every clean dish in the household, for the kitchen counter was stacked high with more dirty dishes than Irene thought she had ever seen.

Was it two hours later that she finally had all the dishes washed, dried, and put away the best she could figure out how? However long it was, she was glad that task was over. Sofia was still not back and Irene looked at the rest of the kitchen. Dirty. That was the only word for it. She swept, wiped countertops, washed the doors that needed it, and at the end found a mop and washed the floor twice.

As she finished, she heard the door open and Sofia walked in. Without a word, Sofia looked at the empty countertop. She walked through the kitchen, looking at the clean cabinet doors and taking in the clean floors and the transformed kitchen.

Irene watched, half afraid she had offended the woman. Maybe in France it was considered an affront for a stranger to clean so much. Would Sofia assume that Irene thought she was a sloppy housekeeper?

"You can see what needs to be done," Sofia finally spoke. "You can actually see what needs to be done without being told!"

Then she told Irene how grateful she was. She began telling her how often the men had tried to find help for her and how that after five girls who were to "help" her had left, Sofia was so frustrated that she had said, "No more!"

Then David had come and told her that Irene was coming to help.

"I said, 'No! I will not have one more person try to help.' But David said, 'It's too late. She already has her ticket and is coming.'

"That night in bed I complained to God. I told Him I was tired of well-meaning, but inept help. I did not want to have one more person come who needed to be told how to work.

" 'Let her come,' God told me.

"Even though I was sure that God was speaking to me, I did not want you to come. I was even upset at God. And now, now I see that He was right!"

All summer long Irene had helped with the housework. She cleaned, cooked, helped with the children, and, yes, was fascinated by the steady stream of people going through the mission.

Bible carriers.

She had heard the stories. Then suddenly she had been asked to take trips into the communist countries.

But I never expected this, she mused as she once more peered fruitlessly through the van window. What if they don't come back? Irene did not want to think about that. What would she do? Were they in prison? Or hurt somewhere and did not know how to tell someone to come and get her? Had they found the address?

It is strange how weak one's faith can get when it is hot and uncomfortable. Discouragement and fear try to raise their ugly heads. There are thoughts and doubts about whether God even cares or is interested in your efforts.

But God did care. The boys showed up as Irene was concluding that she had definitely been abandoned.

"Can't find that address," George shook his head. "Tried to ask people for the street but just got scared looks and shakes of heads. Found one student who spoke a smattering of English, but he was no help."

"The post office! You could ask at the post office," Irene said as the thought flashed into her mind. "The personnel there would surely know."

"Good thinking," Rick said.

George looked at her with respect. Was he going to say "Good thinking for a girl" in his usual teasing way? But no, he was too discouraged and his usual good humor was gone.

"I guess we could try it," he said with a sigh. "Is there anything to eat? All that tramping around made me hungry."

Irene quickly prepared sandwiches. Peanut butter and jelly were becoming the steady fare since they had eaten all the cheese.

"Are you doing all right?" George asked before taking a huge bite out of his sandwich. "You weren't scared, were you?"

Irene smiled slightly. "Yeah, I'm all right, though I was scared sometimes. But God was with me."

"I was praying for you," Rick said. "We were trying to hurry, but nothing worked out, and I kept thinking about you back here by yourself."

"You might have been wondering if we were arrested or something, and you would have to try to get out of here by yourself," George said bluntly.

Irene turned her head and poured water out of the canteen.

"I'm about ready to give up," George said despondently. "Maybe we will just have to take them back with us."

"Let's try Irene's suggestion and find the post office," Rick said as he finished his sandwich. "If we pray and ask God to direct us there, I feel sure we can find the address. You know, the post office is a wonderful idea, even if it comes from the girl who travels with lots and lots of extra clothes." He grinned at Irene and she smiled back.

Their prayers were answered, for indeed, the people at the post office knew just how to direct them to the street they were looking for.

.   .   .   .   .

"No, no, you must stay the night." Irene was almost sure that was what their host was saying. It turned out that a visiting man in the house they had finally found spoke Russian. Since George was fluent in Russian, they could now easily communicate.

Stay the night they did. "We aren't really supposed to," George told Irene and Rick, "but it's late, and since our van is inside their garage and not visible, it should be okay."

For Irene, it was fascinating to be inside a Romanian home. At first she had tried to sort out who was in the family and then found out that, yes, all eight of the children really lived here. Yet they insisted there would be room for them too.

The actual delivery of the Bibles had been somewhat of an anticlimax. There had been no dramatic ending to their trip and no outstanding reception. Just a quick entrance through the yard gate and into the garage.

Irene did not even find out when the Bibles were unloaded and where they were stored. She had been sitting inside, trying to sip a little of the tea that her smiling hostess had given her. It had been a great relief to be able to wash her face, and she felt invigorated and refreshed simply by having found their destination before dark.

Then the village house was suddenly filled with people, and the family's chatter flowed all around her. She desperately wanted to know what was being said. George sometimes remembered and interpreted for Rick and her, and if someone asked her something directly, it had to be interpreted first into Russian and next into Romanian. This made conversation slow and tedious, but when they prayed together before going to bed, there was no need for interpretation. They were all praying to the same God in the name of Jesus. Irene was amazed at how easy it was to pick out that precious name.

Her bed on the sofa offered her very little privacy, but Irene really didn't mind. They had arrived safely with the Bibles. Now she could relax.

Chapter Two

Back Into the Lion's Den

The German-made station wagon hummed smoothly on the eastbound highway, loaded with the usual luggage that accompanies a family going to visit relatives. *Nicolae* gripped the steering wheel with both hands. He leaned tensely forward in his seat.

"It's hard to go back home again, I mean, back to Romania, isn't it?" his wife *Monica* asked. She was sitting in the back seat busily crocheting a scarf.

"Home?" *Betuel* questioned with a laugh, his boyish voice easy and relaxed. The seven years he had spent in Germany had erased any memory of his early childhood in Romania.

Nicolae leaned back and tried to smile naturally. "I know. We still call it home, don't we, Monica? We know that our real home is in Germany. Don't we have passports proving it?"

With his left hand, he felt the passport inside his jacket. It was there, along with Monica's and their son Betuel's. They had to wait for almost the entire seven years of their stay in Germany before the longed-for documents had arrived and they had cut their legal ties with Romania.

Nicolae scanned the horizon in front of him. The seemingly endless road stretched out ahead. The highway was not crowded, for here in Yugoslavia the grip of communism was still in control, although a little more relaxed than the countries to the east.

Then he saw it. The guardhouse, built on stilts, close to the border. He swallowed nervously and felt his heart beat more rapidly. For one wild moment he thought about turning around. Why had he ever gotten into this?

The past loomed before his eyes. He saw once again their desperate flight across the border into Yugoslavia, the guide taking the small group of fleeing Romanians through the night. He remembered with painful clarity the hours of trying to hurry slowly so as not to set off any alarms in the wire-rigged zone between the two countries. The desperation that had caused them to flee had then seemed small compared to the danger of being caught and hauled back into jail, perhaps to rot forgotten and forsaken inside some stronghold.

But they had made it. He and Monica and Betuel. They had left two-year-old *Daniel* with Monica's mother and were later able to get him into Germany.

The memory of their first years in Germany and the feeling of not belonging anywhere wanted to wash over him as he thought of the difficulties they had endured. Now they had a life—a home, a church, and steady income from his job. Life had actually become sane, manageable, and, for the first time, seemingly secure.

Now here he was, headed back into Romania. Back to the lion's den.

"I see the border!" Betuel announced, looking up from his electronic game.

"I'm surprised you noticed," Monica laughed. But Nicolae heard the tension in her laugh and knew that she, too, was remembering.

"I improved my score by twenty!" Betuel said exultantly. "I'm getting better all the time!"

Nicolae hardly heard him. Electronic games were not interesting to him. He once had tried to play a game at Betuel's insistence, but could never seem to make his fingers move fast enough to catch the little figures that scurried across the screen in dizzying swiftness. The hum of the tires on the pavement dropped to a lower pitch as Nicolae stepped on the brakes. A line of cars in front of them waited patiently for their turn.

Nicolae looked in his rearview mirror. No cars behind him. Slightly lowering his eyes, he surveyed their pile of luggage. Suitcases. Boxes. Bags. All the trappings of a family going to visit friends and relatives.

Would the guards be able to tell this was their first time back in Romania? Their names on their passports would be a giveaway of their nationalities, but there was no way they could tell that they had only recently gotten their passports. Oh, yes, the date issued. But there was nothing to indicate that they were different than any other Romanian/German citizen.

Or could the guards check some kind of list to watch out for returning Romanians? With new computer technology, Nicolae wasn't sure. Things were very modern in 1986 compared to seven years ago. He wasn't sure how much information the border guards could access.

"Are you praying?" Monica's quiet voice interrupted his thoughts. Betuel was busy once more with his game.

"Now I am," Nicolae gave a deep sigh and immediately began directing his thoughts to God.

God. His jumbled thoughts began to settle into a reasonable pattern once more. Yes, God was in control.

In his youth, Nicolae had known there was a God. He had seen the power of Jesus Christ in his parents' lives. As a teenager, he had questioned his parents' faith, but God had mercifully shown him his own need and had touched him deeply.

At the university where Nicolae was a student, he had seen the struggle between the ideologies of the state and the deep conviction of the Christians as they openly lived out their faith. He had thrown himself willingly into being a voice for Jesus. The group of students who dedicated themselves to follow Christ kept growing. Along with that came the watchful eye of the authorities and then the usual crackdown.

It had been during this time that he had first gotten involved with transporting Bibles. The need for Bibles had been so acute that he and others would scout the city for leads on where to get the precious book, and whenever a source was located, they quickly exhausted it.

Interest in Bible knowledge continued to grow, and he and a number of others began traveling in order to bring more Bibles into the city. Their travels were monitored by the authorities, and although there was a certain thrill in the cat and mouse game of trying to elude the secret agents, Nicolae never got used to the danger inherent in their Bible smuggling.

Sure enough, he was eventually hauled off to the police station and grilled for information. Thankfully, he could not divulge information that he did not have. So successful were the people involved in not allowing names and addresses to be exchanged that Nicolae had very little to offer.

Placed under house arrest for over a year, Nicolae had at first chafed under the forced restrictions, but eventually he found an outlet as he threw himself into study and memorization.

Finally, he and Monica had decided to leave their country. They had escaped successfully and now, here he was, headed back again. The cars ahead of him slowly moved.

"Thank you, Jesus!" Nicolae felt a surge of joy. He smiled. "Look! There is *Iosif*! Our old neighbor!"

He knew it! This was what he had prayed for! Oh, God was good to him! Nicolae's mind was spinning.

"Why are you so excited to see Iosif?" Monica asked, looking intently at her husband in the mirror.

"He can help us! This is what I wanted!"

"So you did bring them," Monica said quietly. Their eyes met briefly in the mirror.

That had been a disagreement between them. "Let's take the first trip and see how it goes," Monica had said. "We can then prepare better for the next trip."

But Nicolae hadn't listened. He had remembered with what joy the Romanians always received the Bibles. Their faces, intense with the hunger for spiritual food, had come to him vividly. So he had put ten Bibles in a satchel and put it into the back of their station wagon just before he had slammed the door. They were back there right now.

"Our turn!" Betuel looked up from his game as Iosif's car moved forward ahead of them.

They inched forward.

"See, I prayed that I would meet someone I know. Then between the two borders, after the other man's luggage is checked, I can put our bag into their trunk!" Nicolae told his wife.

"How . . . ?" Monica's voice trailed away as they reached the first checkpoint.

Nicolae rolled his window down. The uniformed Yugoslavian guards checked their passports, looked inside their car, and nodded.

Nicolae drove slowly forward. Now they were in no man's land, the strip of land between the countries. Here they waited again. The familiar uniforms of the Romanian guards caused Nicolae to take a deep breath.

"I did it!" Betuel's voice was loud and sharp with glee. "I made it all the way to the next level."

"Betuel!" Nicolae's voice was sharp. "There is more to be concerned about right now than your game!"

Betuel sat back and looked silently out the window.

Ahead of them, they watched as Iosif opened his trunk and the officer checked inside the car, taking his short stick and thumping the back of the car seats. Then the officer left.

In a flash, Nicolae was out. "Iosif!" he called out.

Surprised, the man turned in their direction. Recognition flooded across his face for an instant. But quickly he turned and looked apprehensively toward the small office. All was still.

The two men shook hands, and Nicolae said in a low voice, "Don't close your trunk right away. I have something to put inside. You have already been inspected."

Iosif understood immediately. There were many goods that were difficult to get inside Romania, and it was common to smuggle foreign items across the border. "What is it?"

"Bibles," Nicolae said eagerly.

The friendliness faded from Iosif's face as though a switch had been turned off. Shaking his head, he went swiftly back to his car. Several minutes later when the guard returned, he drove off, not once glancing back at Nicolae.

"Get back in the car!" The officer shouted at Nicolae.

Meekly, Nicolae obeyed. He felt deflated, drained. He could not even pray. His heart began pounding incredibly fast and he could barely swallow.

"Now what?" Monica asked quietly as they watched the officer disappear inside the office again.

Two dogs, well fed and confident, trotted around the corner. They paid no attention to the nervous travelers, but Nicolae knew they would if he tried to do anything unusual.

"I don't know what we'll do. Pray that God would close their eyes, I guess." Nicolae could barely speak.

Betuel's fingers continued to fly as he tried to better his score. "I could hide them under my coat," he said calmly.

Nicolae looked at his son, swaddled in a heavy winter coat. April was still cold and clinging to winter.

"Good idea!" Monica said quickly. "Where is the bag?"

She was on top of the luggage in a flash and drew the bag forward.

"Continue to play the game," Nicolae encouraged, and when Monica passed the paperbacked Bibles forward, he pushed them under Betuel's coat.

"Tuck them inside the waist of your pants. Quick!"

The door of the office opened and the guard came out. He walked toward them. Betuel looked up and rolled down his window as the guard approached the passenger's side.

"Passports," he demanded curtly.

Nicolae passed over the three German passports. Flicking through the booklets, the officer looked at Betuel. "Do you still speak Romanian?"

Betuel smiled and nodded.

"That's good," the guard said approvingly. "Don't ever forget your mother language."

Betuel's fingers tapped his game. "Wanna try my game?" he asked with a boyish grin.

Nicolae couldn't believe his ears. Why was Betuel detaining the officer? Wasn't he conscious of his precarious position, hiding Bibles under his coat? He shouldn't try to detain the officer.

"How does it work?" The officer reached toward the offered game piece.

"See, you control it with this little lever. You try to see how many of the flying objects you can trap. I can get 200 now!" Betuel demonstrated and the officer watched in fascination as the young boy's fingers flew across the keypad.

The guard tried several times, but his attempts were futile. "You are a lot better than I would ever be," he laughed good-naturedly. Then he returned to business, asking Nicolae and Monica to step out of the car. He searched their luggage, stamped their passports, and waved them through!

Total silence filled the car as they passed through the last gate. Then as Nicolae drove steadily on into Romania, the Bibles still safely around his son's waist, he clutched suddenly at his stomach.

"What's wrong?" Monica asked as Nicolae bent forward.

There was no time to answer. Nicolae slammed on the brakes and swerved to the side of the road. He sprang from the car and bent over the ditch as his knotted stomach emptied itself convulsively. With a sweaty brow and trembling legs, he returned silently and got into the car.

"Papa, you were nervous, weren't you?" Betuel was once more focused on his electronic game, skillfully catching the racing forms. "I knew God would watch over us."

"Thank you, son, for the reminder," Nicolae said as he shifted into gear. "I see God has been watching over us in ways I did not imagine."

Monica smiled at him in the mirror and reached forward to touch his shoulder briefly. "I am glad you brought the Bibles even though I thought we shouldn't. I'm sure there will be joyful people receiving the Word they are praying for."

.   .   .   .   .

"Every month you come. Every month you have food for your 'relatives' as you call everyone in Romania, I imagine."

Nicolae nodded pleasantly at the border guard. He waited respectfully for the inspection of the RV to be completed, feeling that familiar tightening in his stomach. He bit into his apple again. "Keep something in your hand that occupies you," a seasoned traveler once told him. "It not only helps you, it somewhat disarms the guards."

Whether it made any difference to the guards, Nicolae did not know, but it surely helped his nerves. Apples were the common choice for him since they were easy to obtain and easy to digest.

"Out!" The guard motioned abruptly and Nicolae complied. "You too," he said to Betuel.

Father and son stood to one side and watched the officer. First he checked under the front seats. He took a small hammer and tap-tapped on the floorboards. Then he opened the side door and said, "Okay, get all the suitcases and boxes out."

The two set to work. Suitcases with their own clothes and bundles of clothes to be given to their Romanian friends. Boxes of food for them to eat along the way and boxes of food for the Romanians. Bags of flour, rice, and several smaller bags of sugar. All stacked inside the RV on the built-in benches, on the floor, and in the storage compartments.

"You guys sure go through a lot of work," the guard complained when all the luggage was finally stacked on the inspection tables.

He hardly looked at the boxes, merely opening them and briefly checking the contents. Then, climbing back inside the RV, he began a methodical inspection of the walls and the ceiling and continually tap-tapped with his hammer, listening intently.

The panel behind the shelf in the back seemed to intrigue him. The now empty shelf was deep, but not very high. He squirmed himself into the shelf and tapped all along the back, listening for a hollow sound. Squirming back out, he fished a screwdriver out of his pack and went back on the shelf again. Taking out screw after screw, he began loosening the panel.

Nicolae saw him through the front windshield. He watched the sturdy boots wave in the empty space of the RV. He counted as the guard moved from space to space taking out the screws.

Five. He had removed five screws. Nicolae's stomach churned. Six.

Betuel's attention was distracted by a heated exchange between two other guards, but Nicolae couldn't keep his gaze from following the guard's progress. Seven screws. He had now removed seven screws. There were no words in Nicolae's desperate prayer. Just a stream of wordless pleas for help kept coming from some deep place inside him.

He remembered the prison when they had first escaped into Hungary. As was the custom, every illegal immigrant crossing the border was immediately held in prison while the officials checked records to make sure no one was a dangerous criminal running from the state. The prison had been crowded. Rough and loud-mouthed men, hardened by years of crime, gave no recognition to anyone else's plight. The three days had stretched into a living nightmare.

But I am a German citizen now, Nicolae tried to rationalize. *I could appeal to my country for help.*

Yeah, right, a voice seemed to snicker. *You think anyone would help you, bringing contraband into this country? Guess again. You would be counted as just another person trying to smuggle in goods. Hundreds of them exist.*

Nicolae knew it was true. Taking hard-to-purchase goods into "closed" countries could make big money. And big money was made. Lots of people knew that.

Even though this particular guard had searched Nicolae's RV before, it would only be a matter of time before he would be moved somewhere else. The "big bosses" knew that many a border guard was bribed to look the other way. Bribed heavily at times.

Nicolae looked at the two bags at the end of the row on the inspection table. He knew what was in there. Coffee. Sugar. Cassette players.

Those two bags were to be left behind as "gifts." He knew it and the guards knew it. They expected it. Were they bribes? Some questioned whether Christians should do that, but most of the criticism came from people who had never navigated the corrupt and dangerous maze of a communist bureaucracy.

Nicolae had to settle the matter in his own conscience. "For anything else, I would not do it," he had told Monica. "But if I can get Bibles into the hands of the waiting people, I will gladly give gifts to the guards."

Eight. Eight screws were removed. Nicolae gnawed at the apple core.

There was a flurry of legs thrashing, and the guard jumped down. He shook his head and stalked out of the RV. "I know you are taking something in. I just know it." He glared at Nicolae for a moment.

Nicolae heard himself say in a voice that seemed not to be his own, "You can search again."

"Pah!" The guard shook his head and walked away. "Put that stuff back in."

Betuel and Nicolae began the tedious task of trying to fit all the boxes back inside. It always seemed harder the second time.

By the time they had their possessions loaded, the two bags on the end had disappeared. That was the way it was supposed to work. As though neither party knew what was happening, yet fully aware of the transaction.

"Papa," Betuel said after Nicolae had taken his usual trek down the grassy bank on the Romanian side, "doesn't it get easier?"

Nicolae wiped his mouth with the back of his hand. He hated that taste that always stayed behind even after his stomach was empty. "Son, I don't think it does."

Betuel was thirteen years old now. He had accompanied his father into Romania more times than he could remember and was a great help on their trips.

"I don't know why," Nicolae said. "I know I trust in God to help us, but there is still always something inside of me that shrivels whenever we are at the border. Like today."

"He almost found it, didn't he?" Betuel asked softly. "I think only God kept him from taking out the last two screws."

Nicolae couldn't speak. His eyes were wet with tears as he nodded.

They rode on together, traveling into the heart of Romania, taking their cargo, following the vision that God had given Nicolae.

The work had picked up in tempo when an American organization had somehow found out about his trips into his homeland. Bibles, literature, and addresses came to his home in Germany, and Nicolae worked long and hard to do his part.

"Do you think the people donating the Bibles realize how hard it is to get the gifts across?" Betuel asked thoughtfully. "Do you think they realize what you go through?"

Nicolae shook his head. "Probably not." He had wondered about that himself. He pictured the people in the West donating money or donating Bibles for their brethren in the East. He had glimpses of even poor people being moved of God to share what little they had in order that others could have God's Word. He knew there were many volunteers who donated hours and hours of their time to package Bibles and arrange them for shipping. And there were printers not charging for their time, so that the work could go forward.

"Our part is only a small contribution to this whole movement," Nicolae told his son. "When the church of Jesus Christ works together, no one seeks recognition for his part. It is all a labor of love."

Betuel nodded. He knew this was true because he saw it in his father's life.

Chapter Three

"He's Sitting on the Bibles"

*P*avel's arms ached. He flexed his muscles and felt spasms grab at his biceps. Even trying to massage the one arm with the other was painful. Looking at his companion, *Dorel*, he knew that his brother felt the same pain.

Abruptly, the loud, shrill whistle of the approaching train galvanized them into action. All across the train station, the waiting people began moving toward the approaching locomotive. With an inward groan, Pavel grabbed the two suitcases and tried not to cry out as pain once more racked his tortured arms and shoulders.

Earlier it had not been too difficult to make it appear that the suitcases he carried were just the ordinary type of luggage a man would take with him on a normal journey. Even though each suitcase weighed more than sixty pounds, both men were strong and able to take the weight well. It had been after their long walk to the train station that the pounds had begun to tell on them.

They had walked more than three miles, not daring to hire a taxi and not knowing anyone well enough to ask for a ride by car. Not with the precious cargo they carried.

"Pray," Pavel murmured nervously to Dorel as the two men inched forward. A brief nod from Dorel acknowledged the request.

When Pavel spotted the two gypsy men lounging behind the corner of the station, he was seized with a sudden idea for getting past the guards. Putting down one suitcase and ignoring the agony in his aching arm, he linked his now free arm around one gypsy man and pulled him along.

"Hey! Whatya doin'?" The protest came quickly.

The other man came swiftly to his buddy's aid. Grabbing Pavel by the other arm, he tried to swivel the big man around.

The shrill whistle of the station guard pierced the noise of the engine idling on the tracks. In no time at all, the station guards swooped into the fray and roughly separated the gypsy men from the two travelers. In their indignant efforts to chase the gypsies from the area, they paid little heed to the two men boarding the train with their heavy suitcases.

The narrow corridor of the train car was difficult to navigate, so Pavel took one suitcase at a time to the middle cabin as Dorel guarded the remaining ones. The train was already in motion, and the two men drew deep sighs of relief as they sat down gratefully on their seats.

It felt so good to rest. The strain of the heavy suitcases and the anxiety they had felt at the station had drained them.

"Thank you, Lord," Pavel said under his breath. He closed his eyes and mentally retraced their journey.

"There are Bibles in the south." The message had come to him through a brother in the church. "Lots of Bibles. Hundreds and maybe even thousands." Details had been sketchy as was often the case. There had been times when similar reports had reached them and Pavel or others had traveled to see if they could get Bibles, but none had been available. This time, however, they had been rewarded.

The sheer number of Bibles had amazed Pavel and Dorel as they stood with gaping mouths in front of the stacked books. Not only were there paperback New Testaments, but complete hardbound Bibles.

"Hundreds of volunteers waded into the water and formed a line, passing Bibles from one to the other," they had been told. "The foreigner's boat had not been allowed to dock, but God somehow opened a way of communication. The people who got the message just came surging out of the city. In the early dawn they waded right into the shallow water and began to work."

There had been no time to press for details. Everyone knew that time was of the essence in order to get the precious cargo out of the garage where they were stored and out of the city.

Thus Pavel and Dorel's journey with the laden suitcases had begun.

That had been yesterday. All night they had traveled, and reaching the station in time to make this train, they were now headed back to *Suceava*.

The train began to slow for a scheduled stop. The lurching car took the jolt of the long line of cars behind them and Pavel heard the squealing of the brakes. The crowd of commuters that boarded the train looked quickly for empty seats, and in several minutes their cabin was filled to capacity. Passengers still continued to appear at the doorway, look in, and move on to search for empty places. The corridor became crowded as many stood in the narrow passageways.

The tall form of a uniformed officer scanning the crowded cabin now loomed in the doorway. Spying the stacked suit-cases that had been too heavy to put in the overhead racks, he entered the cabin and settled himself wearily on top!

All thoughts of rest fled from Pavel's tired body, and his mind began to race. How long would it take until the officer would begin to wonder what was inside these sturdy, heavy suitcases? Would he be able to sense their uneasiness at his unconventional choice of a seat? Should he offer his own seat to the officer and sit on the suitcases? His mind quickly rejected the idea. No, that would only bring attention to himself and Dorel.

Sinking into his jacket, Pavel tried to disappear. He looked out the window as the train once more began to move and watched as the station disappeared from view. The locomotive picked up speed as they once more traveled through the countryside.

Taking sideways glances at the officer, Pavel saw the eyes of the middle-aged man droop as he swayed wearily with the motion of the train. Noticing the insignia on the shoulder of the jacket, Pavel could see the impressive row of colors indicating his high rank.

Pavel felt his spirits droop even lower. His uneasy mind dashed back to when they boarded the train. *God, perhaps I shouldn't have used the innocent gypsies as a cover to get on the train undiscovered. Is this your way of punishing me?*

Deep inside, Pavel knew that God was not out to punish His children who, in spite of their mistakes, were seeking to advance His Word. And yet he struggled. Surely God wouldn't cause others to suffer for his error.

"Lord," Pavel prayed fervently, "you know these Bibles mean

so much to our people. Please let us deliver them safely to the very ones who need them." His mind went to the constant request for Bibles from people in his congregation.

"You have placed it on someone's heart to go to the expense and work of getting these Bibles, and there must be countless people who have been involved in shipping and bringing them to our country. Can you please protect them now and let us take them to our churches?"

His own safety was no longer the pressing concern, although he was well aware of the days and weeks of interrogation that often followed the discovery of Bibles. Then came the prison terms, the torture, and even the murders of those thought especially dangerous to the state. All because they had smuggled Bibles in far smaller quantities than he was now doing.

He had comforted sobbing families after members had been sentenced to years in prison for distributing Bibles. Yes, Pavel was well aware of the dangers. But now his heart was moved more because of the great need to get these Bibles to the people who were waiting for them.

The officer straightened up as the lurching train disturbed his rest. Glancing at his watch, he stretched and leaned back against the window. He studied his fingernails.

Dorel shifted slightly in the seat beside Pavel, and Pavel sensed that his companion was also praying. Praying earnestly and desperately.

The train slowed once more. A few people got off after it stopped at a station, but their cabin remained full. Soon the train started up again.

When the two uniformed officers first appeared at the door of their cabin, Pavel felt his heart plummet once more as he saw their mission. They were security officers doing an unannounced luggage check! This was just one more way the government tried to control the people. One more way of discovering contraband!

The officers' words were brief and terse, but words were hardly needed. The passengers all knew what to do. They promptly and silently opened handbags or whatever they were carrying for the guards' inspection.

Pavel closed his eyes. He tried not to imagine the stir the Bibles would cause as the suitcases were opened and the black books laid open to the eyes of everyone in their cabin.

But when the two searching officers merely saluted their superior officer sitting on the suitcases and bypassed them, Pavel's mouth dropped open in amazement! He hastily shut it again lest his bulging eyes and slack jaw attract attention. The sitting officer acknowledged the two briefly and settled himself more comfortably on his seat.

With great effort, Pavel restrained himself from shouting his praises out loud, but in his heart, praises rang to the heavens. "Thank you, Lord, that you have kept your books safe. I know there are still miles to travel to take them safely home, but I thank you for this sign! I have the assurance that we will have no problems with our cargo. Wow, sitting right on them, and this officer does not have an idea what a solid foundation he is on! And using him to keep them safe from inspection! O, Lord, how good you are. My trust and confidence in you are stronger and surer. Thank you, oh, thank you!"

So great was his joy that after the sleepy officer finally got off the train, Pavel surreptitiously pulled five Bibles from one of the suitcases. To the astonishment of the remaining travelers in their car, he announced, "If there is anyone here who needs a Bible, I have one for you. This is God's Word and there is life in these pages. Read it diligently to understand and discover that Jesus Christ can save your souls and set you free from sin."

Dorel was amazed as his friend, empowered by the Spirit, began to preach to the people. The passengers in the car were equally amazed. What was this man doing? Was he crazy? Could he be drunk? They had not noticed him taking any sips from a vodka bottle.

"Jesus has changed my life. He has given me a new heart that no longer wants to sin. I now seek only to serve Jesus and live for Him. He wants to change the hearts of all people and bring peace and salvation to everyone."

The five Bibles were eagerly accepted. Tears fell freely from the wrinkled cheeks of one elderly lady as she hugged the book to her breast.

Later, when Dorel questioned the wisdom of his actions, Pavel said, "O brother, if you could have felt the tremendous gratitude that swelled up in my heart, you would not question my actions. I felt like the disciples when Jesus spoke to them on the Emmaus road. My heart burned within me."

Dorel nodded. "I agree. I just … well, you know. We have been so secretive and quiet for so long."

Pavel smiled. "I know. Today, at least for that moment, I was moved to break that silence. So strong was the presence of the Spirit that I felt I had to speak or my heart would burst."

"I feel as though my arms will burst if I lift those heavy suitcases one more time," Dorel said with a wry smile. "But here is our station, and I know the Lord will give us strength to carry this heavy load again."

With a groan, Pavel stood, flexing his strong arms and feeling the pain shoot up into his shoulders again. But strangely, or perhaps not so strangely, the pain was not as bad as he anticipated. New strength surged through both men, and they were able to pick up their heavy loads and get off the train without any difficulty.

Though the two men would suffer from sore muscles for a week afterward, the joy that accompanied their mission was well worth any physical pain they needed to endure.

．　　．　　．　　．　　．

Pavel stood in the line at the train station and waited for his turn to purchase a ticket. He sighed deeply, his usual merry face drawn, and the tension he felt was revealed in the lines around his eyes.

"Do not go." God's voice came to him clearly.

Pavel glanced around. But even as he did, he knew he would not see anyone who had spoken to him. This voice came from inside his mind and it was one he had heard before.

"Do not go. This is not your time." The voice was gentle but persistent.

The line ahead of him inched forward. Pavel shuffled his feet to keep his space.

Not go? Not leave his country that persecuted him? Give up escape not only for himself but also for his wife and sons? Why would he not leave a system that punished pastors for caring deeply for their congregations and trying to supply them with Bibles? Why not flee from a system that spied and harassed and made life miserable for anyone who stood for the truth and exposed greed and deception?

But the voice was clear, unmistakable, and insistent. "Do not leave."

Pavel exhaled slowly. He looked at the man behind the ticket window. For him, that man represented freedom. Escape.

Pavel had been abroad. He had traveled to Austria, to Germany, and to England. He had tasted the freedom with which the Christians there operated, and he had enjoyed the heady experience of being out of the reach of the repressive communist regime.

Now pressure against the believers was at an all-time high. Pavel had experienced it personally. He had been arrested for smuggling Bibles on a train, had been interrogated, and then was suddenly released when word of his arrest had leaked out to the West. He found out later that Henry Kissinger, the US Secretary of State, had been notified, and even though he knew little about the man, he had felt extreme gratitude for that influential man's role in his release.

But the constant harassing, the pressure on him and his family—it was too much. Pavel had finally decided to leave.

Yes, he knew that for a while the security police would come and visit his wife and ask her all kinds of questions as they already did when he was not at home. Pavel almost chuckled at the memory of what his wife once did to an officer. A good hostess to all, Maria had served coffee to the interrogator. Strong coffee.

"I guess he couldn't handle much caffeine, because soon he was shaking uncontrollably," Maria had related. "His hands shook so much he could barely write. Finally, he stood up and said, 'I have to leave. I can't think straight. Next time, no coffee.' And the interview was over."

In spite of the humorous memory, Pavel knew the decision

to leave was serious. Only after a long time of prayer had he decided to leave. His friends in Austria had promised they would help get his family out of Romania.

"Do not go." The voice came clearly even as the line in front of Pavel thinned and his turn came closer. A huge shuddering sigh shook his frame as he picked up his suitcase and turned to step obediently out of the line.

As though waiting for that cue, two uniformed security officers approached him, each seizing an elbow, and quickly marched Pavel into a narrow corridor where they unceremoniously pulled him into a room and locked the door behind him. It happened so quickly, so unexpectedly, that Pavel could barely perceive what was going on.

From where had the security police come? Pavel had been in line, waiting to buy his ticket, fighting a battle in his mind, and the moment he had obeyed the voice, he had been grabbed and hustled into this room.

"Where were you planning to go?" The question shot out at him angrily.

"I had planned to buy a ticket, but I changed my mind," Pavel told the interrogator honestly.

"Hah! We changed your mind."

"No, God told me not to leave."

"God doesn't speak to people. You lie."

Pavel shook his head. "No," he said firmly, "that is the truth. I had planned to buy a ticket to Austria, but God told me not to, so I stepped out of line to go home. That is when you grabbed me."

One officer jerked Pavel's hand out and hit the open palm sharply with his rubber truncheon. Pavel cried out in pain as the officer rapidly beat his open palm again and again.

"We know all about you," the other officer hissed through clenched teeth. "This time there will be no one to tell the people in the West where you are. We will not have President Nixon's people calling to ask why you are treated this way."

In spite of the pain of the beating, Pavel suddenly understood. Once more, the communist trap had been set and sprung. He was caught, alone and unprotected, and suddenly he felt fear sweep over him. Was he to die in this place?

It had happened before. Someone had suddenly disappeared and later a report would filter back to the family asking if the papers found on the corpse of some accident victim belonged to their missing family member. Pavel had witnessed this scene more than once and had prayed with the survivors.

But the pain from the severe beating now traveled up his arm and into his torso, driving away rational thoughts. He was flung onto the floor as the two officers beat him unmercifully, standing on his body to restrain him.

"Lord Jesus! O Jesus! Help! Help me!" Pavel's cries infuriated the two men and they intensified their beating.

Pavel lost track of time. He was only aware of the intense pain that coursed through his body. He tried to shield his stomach and his face.

Finally the beating stopped. The only sound in the room was the heavy breathing of the officers and the moans that came from the form on the floor.

"There will be more of that if you don't stop your activities," the leading officer said after a moment. "Get out of here!"

Pavel tried to rise. He wanted to get out, but his legs did not support him. He slumped back on the floor again. Rough hands grabbed him, pushed him out into the corridor and hustled him out a side door into the daylight. The door slammed shut behind him.

Stumbling across the alleyway, Pavel collapsed on a park bench. A young boy, trotting alongside his mother, looked at him curiously. With a sniff of disdain, the woman hurried her son away. Pavel realized the people must think he was a drunk who had gotten beaten up in a fight. He wanted to go home, but he had to rest and try to get his breath again.

. . . . .

"Sign this." The words were cold and blunt.

Pavel tried to read the words on the paper in front of him.

"… in possession of illegal substance …" That would be the Bibles they had found in his house.

"… attempt to cross the border illegally …" That would be the day he had been beaten in the train station.

"… criminal activities against the state." Yes, he was being charged as a criminal, an enemy of the people.

A blow to the back of his neck, just above his hairline, jerked Pavel's head violently forward.

"Sign the paper." A pen was pushed into his hand.

"I am not guilty." Pavel tried to speak firmly, but the weak sound that came out was barely recognizable even to himself.

Although he had returned home after the beating at the train station, Pavel had been constantly followed and had now been summoned to the police station.

When he still made no move to sign the paper, someone struck him so sharply from behind that his head smacked on the desk in front of him. Literally seeing stars, Pavel slumped off the chair and onto the floor, strength ebbing from his body.

The cursing officer grabbed him by the hair and shoved him back into his chair again. "Sign the paper!"

This time the officer grabbed Pavel's hand, and holding it firmly, he took the pen and forced Pavel's signature onto the document. Then he pushed the beaten man out of the office and onto the street.

· · · · ·

Wearily, Pavel turned and locked the door to the church house. It was late and the last people had left. The darkness outside was but dimly broken by streetlights, shining in intervals except where the bulbs had burned out.

He was tired. The constant harassments, the beatings, and the interrogations had definitely taken a toll on his physical wellbeing.

But again the loving Holy Spirit sent from God restored his inner man, the one that really mattered, bringing peace to his heart. True, Pavel had wrestled with the usual questionings as to why God had kept him in Romania and why he had not been allowed to leave. Yet his faith in his God was stronger than his questions, so as he yielded to the will of God in spite of the persecutions, Pavel once more had found the peace and joy that God gives to His children.

Not only was Pavel willing to obey the voice of the Lord, he began to rejoice once more in the work he was given to do. Preaching to the people who came to the meetings, counseling with the needy, and praying for the sick and elderly, Pavel felt that his work was truly rewarding.

Now, heading down the sidewalk toward his car, Pavel was pleasantly tired.

"Pavel," a voice called softly from the shadows.

He stopped. "Yes?"

"Do not look. Right here, between these two houses, I am leaving a gift for you. Please stay there until I have time to leave."

The voice was a man's voice. A young man.

He nodded slightly, standing under the street light. He waited.

There was a rustling in the darkness and the footsteps faded away.

Pavel stepped off the sidewalk and his shoes brushed against an object. He bent over and his fingers found the handle of a suitcase. He lifted it. It was heavy. Pavel grasped it firmly and returned to the sidewalk, got in his car, and went home.

The suitcase was full of Bibles. Russian Bibles. As Pavel and his wife looked at those books in their darkened home, they lifted their heads and gazed deeply into each others' eyes.

"This is why we were not supposed to leave Romania," Pavel said simply. "God still has work for us to do here."

Maria nodded, even though there were tears in her eyes.

Together they knelt and began to pray.

Pavel never left Romania while it was still under communism. Although closely watched and often interrogated, he continued to help transport Bibles whenever he was asked. Romanian Bibles were distributed in the local churches, and Russian Bibles were sent eastward on their way to the Soviet Union. Many people in the West have heard of this courageous family and since freedom came, Pavel has traveled to various countries, telling their story.

Chapter Four

Bread in Room 107

*S*ilviu opened the door of the second-floor dormitory. He stuck his head into the dimly-lit corridor and looked cautiously in each direction. Stepping outside, he motioned to his two friends, Dorel and *Romică*, to follow him.

The three moved noiselessly down the hall, and without exchanging as much as a whisper, they glided down the stairs on nimble feet.

The stairs led to the hall on the first floor of their dormitory. The double front doors leading onto the grounds of the university were locked, but it was a simple matter for the three young men to turn the knob from inside and slip out into the night.

Even before they descended the three steps to ground level, they heard the click of the lock behind them. It was a slip lock that automatically locked and kept anyone from entering without a key. Feeling inside his pocket, Silviu's fingers found the metal key. Although he had checked for that key several times before exiting his room, he needed to reassure himself once more.

Once they were on the sidewalk, leaving the cluster of university buildings behind, the boys breathed a little easier, but still hurried. The autumn air was chilly, and clouds scudded across the waxing quarter moon.

"You have the money." Romică's statement was almost a question.

"Yes," Silviu responded promptly. "Enough for three tickets."

"We'll have to pull our belts in tighter next week," Dorel predicted as they rapidly walked three abreast. "It will be thin soup again, I think."

Silviu merely nodded. They were close to the train station.

The train ride from Bucharest to *Constanța* lasted almost three hours, and as soon as the three arrived at their destination, they went right out into the night. Silviu checked the huge clock outside the station. One o'clock. They were right on time.

With a wave, Silviu beckoned a waiting taxi. In spite of the extra expense, he wanted to get to their meeting place as quickly as possible.

"Stop right here, please," Silviu requested of the driver a short time later. They pulled up to the curb next to some apartment buildings. Many of the entrance doors had no light at all, while here and there a feeble bulb struggled to illuminate the apartment numbers.

"Have a good time," the driver joked after Silviu paid him and he began to pull away from the curb. He laughed as he sped away.

Silviu glanced cautiously up and down the shadowy street.

"Leave your bags here and keep walking," a man's muffled voice came from a darkened entrance. "Come around again in ten minutes to pick up your bags."

The boys dropped their canvas carry bags and moved on into the night. Silviu shivered and forced himself not to scrutinize the area too closely. The shadows of the night loomed dark around him, and he shivered involuntarily.

He knew he would be expelled from the university if he was caught. It had not been easy to gain admission to one of the best schools in Romania, but he was a good student and had done well on the entrance exams. He knew his companions would face the same fate if they were caught roaming the streets of Constanța in the middle of the night. Their identification cards clearly indicated that they were university students in Bucharest. They would have no reasonable excuse if they were stopped and questioned by any policeman.

But deep inside, Silviu knew they were doing the right thing. So great was the need to get Bibles into the hands of the believers and, perhaps even more importantly, into the hands of the students who were earnestly seeking for truth and meaning in their lives, that it was well worth taking the risk.

When they returned to the spot where they had left their empty sacks, they saw the dim outline of bags now filled with books. Without exchanging a word, the three boys each took two heavy bags and silently hurried back toward the train station.

This time they did not hire a taxi. Their luggage would have been enough to raise questions, and taxi drivers knew they could reap a reward for reporting suspicious activity to the police.

At first the bags did not seem very heavy. Block after block they walked rapidly. If they missed this train, they could never get back in time to attend their first classes.

The weight of the Bibles seemed to increase as the young men hastened toward their destination. No time to stop and rest, no time to gain a moment's respite for their aching shoulders; they could only go on. Determinedly, they pressed forward.

．　．　．　．　．

"Thank God, we made it!" Dorel gasped in relief as the three hurried on board.

"If those tramps hadn't started a fight just as we got to the train station, we could still have been in trouble." Silviu flexed his fingers, looking down at the heavy bags in the compartment with them.

"Not many people traveling tonight," Dorel said, putting his head back and closing his eyes.

At the next train stop the boys heard a babble of women's voices outside the train. Then two middle-aged ladies came on board. The train was already moving by the time they reached the compartment where the boys were.

"Number twelve. Is this number twelve?" one of the women asked.

"Yes, it is," Dorel replied.

"Then this is our cabin." The woman turned to her companion. "*Lucia,* bring your bags in here."

Silviu reached out to help the speaker with her bag, but she ignored him and pushed the bag overhead onto the shelf. Sitting down, she hugged her canvas carryall to her breast.

Lucia came in and she, too, had two bags. She easily swung her carry-on bag overhead. Turning to her companion, she said briskly, "*Lila*, give me your bag. You don't want to hold it all the time."

Glancing sideways at the boys, Lila furrowed her brows.

"They are not going to take it," Lucia sniffed. Looking at the bags between the boys' feet, she added knowingly, "They have their own bags."

The two newcomers settled themselves and looked curiously at the boys. Lucia broke the silence by asking, "Where are you boys going? To the army?"

Dorel spoke up quickly, "Oh, no. We are university students. Going back to our university."

"So what's in your bags?" Lucia asked bluntly.

The silence was broken only by the rhythmic sound of the train wheels underneath them.

"Bread," Romică said simply.

"That's right, bread," Dorel confirmed with a chuckle. Silviu smiled inwardly as he thought of how true the boys' answer was. "I am the bread of life," Jesus had said in John 6:35.

"Oh, you poor boys," Lila sympathized in a lowered voice. "I imagine you hardly get enough to eat in your university. I think it is terrible how difficult our times are. Not enough bread in the cities, and to think we have to travel to the villages to get bread!" She clapped her hand over her mouth and looked sheepishly at her companion.

"It doesn't matter, Lila," Lucia said in her blunt manner. "I don't care if they know that we also left Bucharest to buy bread. Lots of people do that. And if we are searched, believe me, the police will know why we are doing it." She sniffed in disdain and settled back in her seat.

The boys smiled agreeably and nodded their heads.

· · · · ·

Silviu set his bags down outside the dormitory entrance and fished in his pocket for the key. Softly he unlocked the door and stepped aside to let Romică and Dorel go in first. Then he picked up his bags and followed his companions, easing the door shut with one shoulder as he passed inside.

They did not run up the steps as they usually did when they came back from classes during the daytime. Their steps dragged as they carried their precious, heavy luggage up the staircase, one step at a time. Silviu thought longingly of his waiting bed. The hour and a half remaining before the first class started would allow them to get at least a little rest.

The sound of noisily ripping fabric jerked him to attention. With a clatter that sounded loud enough to wake the entire dormitory of sleeping boys, the Bibles poured out from the torn bottom of his canvas bag and began clattering down the metal stairs. Quickly setting down his other bag, Silviu scrambled down the steps to stop the tumbling books.

A muffled exclamation from his friends came down the steps. "Go on up!" he hissed. "Go quickly! No need for all three of us to get caught!"

Making a quick decision, he stacked the scattered Bibles on the sides of the steps. Grabbing his other bag, he darted up the stairs two at a time.

All three boys shoved the bags under their beds and sat breathlessly in their room. Silviu listened intently for any footsteps in the corridor outside.

Dorel opened the door softly and peered out. He shook his head slightly, and as their breathing returned to normal, Silviu said, "Quick. Give me an empty bag and I'll go get the rest."

All was silent except for the pounding of his rapidly beating heart as the young man went down the stairs and retrieved the Bibles.

Lying wide awake in his bed in spite of the sleepless night, Silviu retraced their night's adventure. "Lord Jesus, thank you. I know we don't deserve it, but we do thank you that you protected us and kept your Bread safe. Now guide us by your Spirit to contact the right people who need your Word." His prayer merged into dreams as he fell asleep.

.   .   .   .   .

"Where did you get your Bible?" one of the university students asked Silviu.

"It was in Classroom 107."

"Just like that?" The girl was curious. "How did it get there?"

Silviu smiled at her. Others in their Bible study group quieted down when they heard the question.

The university lawns spread out around the buildings. Sunshine warmed the spring air and the entire campus was dotted with groups of students taking advantage of the warmer weather.

"That is probably a good question," Silviu replied. "It's one that I can't really answer, but I do have some ideas. I have heard that there are Christians in the West who have a burden to provide Bibles to our countries. So I am thinking my Bible comes from someone who has had a longing to see the Word of God in our hands."

"I wish I had a Bible," the young lady said wistfully, and her sentiment was echoed by most in the group that met occasionally for discussions on religion.

"I would advise you to check Room 107 occasionally to see if there are Bibles available."

"But how … ?" The question was never completed.

"Let's say God provides bread for the hungry," Romică replied with a smile.

The group nodded.

Silviu's eye caught sight of a man clumsily wielding a scythe on the bank beside the road. Silviu studied him for a moment. The middle-aged man took another swing at the grass. Instead of making a neat swath, the grass caught at the blade and tangled into a jumbled mess. Something about his manner seemed rather unusual. He didn't look at all like the farmers back in Silviu's village, where most of the men could effortlessly swing the scythe for hours. This man stopped often and seemed out of breath. Silviu noticed that he stared frequently in the direction of the little group of students.

Silviu forgot the man as they began to pray. He thanked God for the hunger and thirst that many of the students had for knowledge about Jesus Christ. This hunger was one of the reasons Silviu had been willing to help transport Bibles. There was an eagerness among the student body for knowledge of God and of salvation through Jesus.

"Hey! It's starting to rain!" someone cried out as huge drops fell from the sky.

Looking up, Silviu saw a dark cloud directly overhead. Laughing and gathering up their books, the group ran for the shelter of a grove of trees nearby.

"No rain over there," someone pointed to a slope between two buildings. The group left the shelter of the trees and, sure enough, when they got to their destination, the grass was dry and the sun even shone weakly through the edges of the cloud.

"That is amazing! Look, it's still raining over where we were!"

The rest of the group turned back to their discussion, but something had caught Silviu's eye. What was that car doing, parked at the spot where they had been praying minutes before? Why was the form of the man coming out of the car rather familiar? Even at this distance, there was something about him …

Ahh! The man who had been cutting the grass with the scythe, or rather, trying to cut the grass. Yes, he was definitely the one. And the other two men with him were policemen. Silviu knew that.

Rescued! Delivered by the rain!

A feeling of awe came over Silviu as he gazed heavenward at the quickly vanishing cloud. God had sent that cloud, laden with rain, to get them to move to another place before the policemen arrived. Silviu was convinced that the first man had been a spy trying to locate where their group was meeting. Obviously, he had gone off to notify the police.

With a wildly beating heart, Silviu watched as the three men clustered together for a minute or so, looking at the crowded campus. It seemed there was some kind of disagreement, for the two uniformed men left rapidly, and the other man stood staring after them. Turning his head, he glanced once more at the groups of students all over the huge lawn. Then he looked resentfully up at the last remnant of the cloud.

"I hope, Lord, he sees your hand in this," Silviu prayed silently. "I sure do. You are a totally awesome God."

Chapter Five

Inside and Underground

"*Eugen*, are you ready?" Gicu's voice rang out in the early morning.

"You haven't eaten yet," Eugen's mother said swiftly. "Here, take this bread with you. And a little cheese."

Eugen grabbed the food, and picking up his tuba, he went swiftly out the door.

The Aro was already crowded. Gicu was the driver. Sammi and Iosif were in the back seat of the rugged vehicle, and packed among them were the instruments of their band.

Eugen took the front seat. He held his tuba on his lap, the huge horn almost filling the front right up to the windshield.

"Pack these in," Iosif said as soon as they had left their village.

Eugen took the small packages and put as many as he could deep into the throat of his instrument. Then he took his polishing cloth and pushed it in last, hiding all evidence of the packages.

"Everything full?" he questioned.

"Yes," Gicu answered.

The countryside looked peaceful enough as the four traveled together on this Sunday morning. Traveling to sing at an outdoor wedding that was scheduled in a small village, the group was eager to use this method of transporting the Bibles that had been stored for over a month.

Living just outside *Sibiu*, Eugen had been among the youth of his church who had greatly benefited by literature that had come into Romania in the aftermath of a devastating flood. Foreign aid had come pouring into the country and along with it, Christian literature.

The tracts written by Richard Wurmbrand had talked about filling the emptiness in your heart with Jesus Christ. Eugen had been amazed at the clarity and depth of the literature. As a university student, his mind was hungering for solid Biblical teaching and here was an entire gold mine. The youth spent hours copying the tracts and passing them around.

Then Romanian Bibles had turned up by the score. Eugen had been glad to help distribute them.

"We can put them inside our musical instruments!" Iosif had told the other three. "Think how hollow some of them are. Eugen's tuba for instance. And the drums. Completely hollow!"

They had legitimate reasons to travel. They sang at weddings and other special events. What a cover to take Bibles and literature along to outlying places!

"First checkpoint," Sammi said as they approached Sibiu.

The officer on duty watched as cars approached from both directions. The white stick swinging out toward the vehicle meant the driver had to pull off to the side and stop. No one ever knew if they were going to be singled out for inspection. The random searches were meant to keep control over what was being transported.

Eugen prayed silently, knowing the other boys were praying too. They didn't have Bibles or literature every time they traveled, but this morning they certainly did. He was very conscious of the tuba, stuffed with Bibles, on his lap. Where the other Bibles were, he wasn't sure, but there were probably some inside the hollow drum. They had done that before.

When the stick waved them to one side, Eugen shifted the heavy metal instrument slightly to the right.

"The singers," the officer said as he approached their vehicle. "Get out."

They were going to be searched. Obediently, Gicu switched off the engine and everyone got out. Eugen held his tuba in his arms and slipped the shoulder strap over his head.

"Stop!" the officer shouted loudly, pointing to an approaching car. He strode into the middle of the road, waving his stick menacingly. The driver slowed abruptly, and the officer began shouting at him.

The four boys were not idly standing by in the meantime. They tugged their instruments from the vehicle, and Gicu began softly playing music on his violin.

It took some time for the officer to write a ticket and fine the other driver. By the time he returned to inspect the Aro, the boys were waiting patiently and the pleasing notes from the violin gently swirled around them.

"I know you have something in here," the officer grumbled as he began checking their vehicle. He was still visibly upset about the other man's offense. He thumped the hard seats and with his stick explored under the seats. Brushing aside the tire jack, he went all over the interior, checking everything meticulously.

Perhaps it was the peacefulness of the warm Sunday morning, or maybe even the soft notes of the violin that mellowed the officer. He finished his search and, looking at the quartet, said, "Give me a drum stick and I will drum for you."

Sammi said, "Sure," and pulled out the wooden stick. He handed it over to the officer.

Waving his left hand in slow motion to the music, the officer began beating the drum with his right. The low sound filled out the melody Gicu was playing.

Eugen shifted his tuba in his arms. He ran his hand nervously over the smooth metal. What would he do if the officer asked him to join in?

"I will come and play in your group," the officer joked when the melody was over. He handed the baton to Sammi and, with a wave, indicated they could leave.

They repacked themselves into their vehicle and left the control area.

"Then sings my soul, my Saviour God to thee, how great thou art, how great thou art." Gicu began the well-known hymn and the others joined in, singing in harmony. They did not need their instruments. Their voices rose above the noise of the motor as they continued toward their destination.

"That was a miracle," Sammi declared after they had finished the chorus exultantly. "That drum sounded just like it was supposed to. It sounded hollow!"

"Were there—did you?" Eugen began asking, but he knew the answer. Yes, Sammi had filled the inside of the drum with Bibles. The officer had been playing right on top of the Bibles he was looking for and did not even suspect it!

It was a joyful group that arrived at the wedding that day and put the prized books into the hands of the elders of the church. Perhaps no one present knew just why the boys sang and played so well that day. But they knew, and with hearts overflowing, they led the singing with vigor and praise. *

· · · · ·

Just outside of Cluj, the mountains rise to swelling heights and look down over the city. Not steep, not immensely high, but their presence definitely holds a commanding part of the landscape. In the night they loom on the eastern horizon, punctuated only by an occasional light, such as the headlights of a car winding up the road.

Eugen was in a car along with six others. It was not a large SUV with plenty of room, but just an ordinary car, filled to capacity with men. Jammed tightly side by side, they could barely move in the back seat. The driver in the front was given as much elbowroom as possible, but he, too, was jammed against the door, making it awkward to steer.

They had the road to themselves. No one was even walking along the road, and as they turned near the crest, the lights of the city twinkled below them. They turned left off the paved road and bounced quickly along a stony road across the open meadows where herders grazed their cattle, sheep, and goats during the day.

It was hot inside the car, though all the windows were rolled down. Hot because of the crowded conditions and hot because of the summer heat that had not disappeared after sundown. Sweat beaded on the foreheads of the men, and Eugen felt his shirt stick to his back that was jammed against the back of the seat.

"Needs new shocks," someone commented as the car jolted over a rough spot.

* **Publisher's note:** *We do not endorse musical accompaniment in New Testament worship, but found this story noteworthy.*

"Heavy load," someone else remarked tersely.

Eugen peered out the front the best he could. The head-lights picked the way along the road following the side of the mountain.

When the car stopped about fifteen minutes after leaving the highway, everyone exited gratefully. Eugen stretched his arms over his head, and even though the air was clammy, it was a lot better outside in the night than inside that car.

Silently the group of men followed their leader up a single track. No one used a flashlight, but the path was familiar to the man in the front. The others could simply follow the dark shapes ahead of them.

The small cabin at the end of their trek was not unlike scores of other cabins that dotted the mountainside. They had been built as shelters for the herders if they got caught in storms or needed a place to stay overnight. More recently, these cabins had been used by hikers and tourists as overnight shelters.

This cabin had been built years ago, the log sides showing gaps in the chinks. The wooden floor was built of rough-cut boards somewhat smoothed by years of use. Barely twelve feet square, it was by no means spacious. Sparsely furnished with a table, several chairs without backs, and a simple closet with two doors, the cabin squatted on the hillside.

But the men did not spread out on the floor and sleep, al-though it was well after midnight. There was a sense of ur-gency among them.

"We need a place close to Cluj so we can safely store Bibles and literature until someone heads east," Pavel had told the small group of ten men some days before. "Some place out of the city."

Eugen had been among that group. He was still active in distributing Bibles even though he had graduated from the university by now.

Being involved in moving Bibles was not like a job. It was not something you did every day from eight in the morning until five at night. It was not something you got paid to do. There could be long stretches of time when you went about your work and daily life and did nothing. Then, there were times when Bibles needed to be transported and the short nights were filled with long trips. At times the couriers became exhausted by the extra work, and they found it difficult to function at their regular jobs.

Eugen knew. He had been involved in the work for more than seven years. He knew about the "on again, off again" schedule of the people in the work. So when an elder in the church had made an announcement to a trusted group of men one evening, Eugen was all ears.

"We have a place that we think will work," the speaker had said, "but it will take many people to prepare the space."

He had gone on to tell them about the plan. Up on the mountainside he owned a herder's cabin. He had checked and found it possible to dig a tunnel under the cabin and hollow out a spot behind the cabin to store Bibles. He would need ten men to help. Strong men. Men willing to work hard to pick and shovel through the stony ground and carry the dirt down the mountainside far enough to leave no sign of dirt disturbed.

So here they were, ready to begin at last. Taking up several boards, the men set to work. Two by two, the first workers swung their picks. Then they stood aside as two more shoveled the loose dirt into waiting bushel-sized baskets.

"Follow me," the leader said to the four men who gripped the two loaded baskets, and he set off down the mountainside. The last worker followed the five down the slope.

"Here. Dump the dirt right here." In the darkness, Eugen, who was one of the carriers, could see the wave of an arm.

"This will be our garden," the voice in the darkness said. They dumped their baskets and all except one worker returned to the cabin. The remaining man began spreading the dumped soil with a shovel.

At the cabin two other baskets were already loaded. The empty baskets were set down and the four men took the loaded baskets down the mountainside.

Overhead, the crescent moon dimly outlined the working figures ascending and descending the slope. It shone on the elderly man smoothing out the soil. Eventually clouds covered the moon and a nighttime shower of rain fell.

Eugen, now taking a turn at the pick, heard the rain on the roof and was glad for the slightly cooler breeze coming in the open door. But the cabin was still hot and sticky. His clothes were completely drenched with sweat.

They tried to work swiftly, taking turns in order to share the most difficult work. By far the most difficult task was transporting the soil down the slope in the dark. Trying to keep the basket level and having one man walk beside the narrow path was not easy. A stone, unseen in the dark, could trip up a step, and if dirt did spill, it had to be carefully scooped up in the dark lest daylight should reveal any disturbance.

Morning comes early in the summertime, so as soon as the first faint streaks of light came up over the mountains, the men began the task of shutting down their work. All dirt had to be swept up and the floorboards replaced. The baskets had to be carefully brushed out so there was no evidence of any fresh dirt in the cracks. And of course, down at the "garden" site it had to look like a garden, not like a dumping place for soil.

The car was just as jammed on the way out as it had been on the way in. The men were even hotter and, of course, more tired than they had been on the way up. The road was just as rough and jarring.

Inside the vehicle all was quiet. Each man seemed lost in his own thoughts.

Eugen felt his muscles ache. His head wanted to droop and his eyelids felt heavy.

.   .   .   .   .

It took several full nights of hard labor to excavate the cave. They had to stagger their work nights in order to avoid suspicion and to provide rest for the hardworking men. When the cave was completed, it was lined with boards to keep the soil from collapsing. The garden was planted and grew bigger after several weeks. They began storing Bibles in the tunnel.

It proved to be a valuable way station for hundreds of Bibles, both Russian and Romanian. Eugen did not always know when or by whom the cave was emptied.

The security police knew something was up. Just how they found out, Eugene did not know, but they began watching the mountainside.

Close to the cabin was an abandoned mill. The lone hermit who lived there had a terrible reputation, and many of the locals said he was crazy. A pack of vicious dogs patrolled the ramshackle place.

One day the police tried to raid the mill. The dogs attacked them, and even though the police shot and killed one dog, the hermit put up so much resistance that even the police became intimidated and left. Eugen felt sure the police believed there was collaboration between the Bible smuggling and the hermit and that they thought the Bibles were stored in the mill.

So the little cabin continued to be an innocent little hut during the day and a beehive of activity at night when Bibles arrived. The work was done swiftly and quietly. God blessed the efforts of the people and not once did the searching officers find the secret hiding place.

Chapter Six

The Wolves Have Gathered

"*Mark 10:13?*"

Gheorghe clearly heard the voice from the corridor even though the front door to his apartment was only open a crack.

"And they brought young children to him, that he should touch them ..." Many times Gheorghe had asked himself why that particular verse was used as an identification point, but it was always his way of knowing that Bible couriers had arrived.

"*Codrean?*" Gheorghe inquired.

"Yes," his visitor replied matter-of-factly.

Gheorghe opened the door and stepped aside.

Without speaking, the stranger smiled and shook Gheorghe's hand warmly.

Gheorghe closed and locked the door. He escorted his visitor down the hall and into the tiny living room.

"Lucia, come," he called to his thirteen-year-old daughter. "I need you to interpret for us."

As Luci, his oldest daughter, came out of the kitchen where she had been helping her mother, Gheorghe spoke in Romanian, "Welcome to our home and may the peace of God be on your life."

Luci translated the words with ease and then listened as the visitor replied in English.

"He says he is happy to be here. God has given him a safe and prosperous journey."

The tantalizing smell of good food drifted from the doorway leading to the kitchen. "Come, we will eat," Gheorghe said as he led the way.

As they ate, Gheorghe and his guest visited, with Luci capably translating their conversation.

"How is it that you began this work?" Codrean asked.

All the Bible smugglers were known to Gheorghe simply as "Codrean." He wondered how many Codreans he had met in the course of his work with secret Bible distribution.

"It was in 1973 just after I had finished speaking at our evening church service," Gheorghe reminisced. "A foreigner came to me and spoke. I did not understand him and just shook my head, but he didn't leave. He just smiled and followed me around. Even though I was a little uneasy about it, I kept smiling back at him. I think he tried several different languages, but none of them was Romanian."

Codrean was all ears as Luci translated. Gheorghe studied him. There was something about this Codrean that put him at ease. Often the Codreans were in a hurry, wanting to unload their packages and leave. This Codrean seemed very interested in their personal lives. Besides, there was an immediate connection in their spirits, in spite of the language difficulty. "Speak freely to this man," the Spirit whispered to him. "The people in the West need to know."

Gheorghe continued, "Finally I found a brother who spoke German and asked him to find out what this man wanted. It turned out he had a wonderful story to share.

"He said that on the way to Romania from his home in Austria, he received a vision from God in which he saw the face of a man he was to seek in Romania. That night at the church service when he saw me for the first time, he knew I was the man in his vision. I guess that is why he did not go away even after we could not speak together.

"I knew this was from God. When he told me he had something for me, and it turned out to be twenty Romanian Bibles, I was deeply moved. He told me it was entirely up to me, but that if I wanted to be involved in the work, Bibles would continue to come my way.

"And that is how it started."

Codrean's eyes filled with unshed tears as he listened to Luci's interpretation. He nodded and reached across the table to warmly grasp Gheorghe's hand.

"Are you in danger presently?" Codrean's voice was sympathetic.

Gheorghe sipped his soup before answering. "I don't know for sure, but the police are suspicious." He glanced toward the curtained kitchen window of their third floor apartment. "I have been taken to the police station for questioning."

There was a brief silence.

Everyone knew of the danger they were facing. Word had trickled back to Gheorghe that the first Codrean had been killed in a car accident in Austria. Gheorghe felt strongly that someone had found out about the man's connection to the Bible projects and he had actually been murdered. Communist secret agents were known for their expertise in staging just such traffic "accidents."

"Yet you continue," Codrean said.

"Yes," Gheorghe replied. "God has given me the assurance that He wants me to do this work. For five years He has protected me."

"Tell him about the phone that was offered to you," his wife *Lidia* urged him.

Gheorghe shrugged. Then as Codrean lifted inquiring eyebrows, he said, "Oh, someone approached me from the telephone office and told me that since I have been a pastor for so long, I would be able to get a phone. I declined, since I felt strongly that they wanted to tap my line in order to keep better control over what happens here."

Codrean nodded and looking at Luci, he asked her a question.

Luci smiled shyly and answered briefly in English. Codrean asked another question.

Glancing at her parents, Luci began speaking softly. After a while, she turned back to her father. "He was asking if I am a Christian and how I came to believe."

"Oh, you must tell him the whole story," Gheorghe urged. "Just tell him everything. I sense in my spirit that this man was sent to us to encourage us and to let the believers in the West know what God is doing here."

As Luci obediently turned to their guest and began to speak, Gheorghe drew a deep breath and let his mind run back to the beginning of his own walk with the Lord.

He had been in a room at the factory where he was employed as a security guard. Feeling burdened, he had been praying and asking God to reveal Himself to him.

Though not particularly religious, he had been taken to church faithfully all of his young life. After he became a teenager, he had quit going. He had gotten married, and other interests overtook him. Lately though, something seemed missing. His job was not fulfilling, and when Luci was born, his wife's health had suffered. Now he felt empty and unfulfilled and was calling again on the God he remembered from his childhood.

That was when his room had been filled with light and Jesus had stepped inside.

He could tell that Luci was telling this part of the story, for Codrean nodded as he looked at Gheorghe.

Would Luci tell Codrean about Lidia's resistance to her husband's newfound faith?

Yes, for Codrean glanced at Lidia where she sat at the end of the table, her fingers playing with the handle of her tea cup.

Luci's voice faltered and choked with emotion, and Gheorghe knew their daughter was telling about the time when God healed her mother. Gheorghe's own eyes clouded with memories of that emotional time.

Soon after their second daughter Claudia was born, Lidia had become very ill. Gheorghe had left reluctantly to attend church, and Luci and the baby were at home alone with their sick mother. When Lidia's cries of pain had reached Luci in her sleep, the four-year-old girl had jumped up and hastened to her mother's bedside. "I am dying," the mother gasped to her daughter. "Please get help!"

Gheorghe could recite exactly the prayer that little Luci had prayed that day. "Lord Jesus, I am a little girl. I have a little sister, Claudia. If Mama dies, who will feed the baby? Heal my mama, Jesus! I know you can do it."

Lidia told him later, "I felt something like electricity go from the top of my head to the bottom of my feet. I felt relief immediately. I knew that God had done a miracle in my body through my little girl's prayer."

That is when Lidia became a believer and joined her husband in his faith. Together they made a solemn promise to serve the Lord and do whatever He asked of them.

"What a story," Codrean said huskily when Luci finished her narrative. "Praise to the Lord for His wonderful works."

Glancing at the clock on the wall, Codrean said, "I think I should leave."

"We will pray first," Gheorghe said, and they all rose and began to pray. The Romanian prayers mingled with the English one as they thanked God for His goodness and pled for guidance and safety in the work still ahead of them that night.

"Tell Codrean to follow our car and to especially watch for my turn signal," Gheorghe said. "If I turn right or left, he will have to be ready at a moment's notice. If I think we are being followed, I will make many turns to shake off the police."

Nodding, Luci interpreted the words to Codrean. She took her jacket from a hook and joined her father in the hall. Luci was a great encouragement to Gheorghe. More than a translator, she had an active faith and was always willing to cheerfully assist in the work whenever she could. Her simple faith often challenged her parents' own trust in God.

·   ·   ·   ·   ·

"Turn left."

Obediently, Gheorghe pulled the turn signal lever down and made a hasty left. Glancing in his mirror, he saw the headlights of Codrean's car close behind.

"Turn right."

It would not have been easy to explain to anyone just how he knew when and where to turn. The voice that came to him at the right time had to be the Holy Spirit. Gheorghe did not question the directions. He simply obeyed even if he did not see anyone trailing them.

Perhaps more than anything, he had learned to trust the guidance of the Spirit in this matter. This was God's work, and surely God was giving the guidance. They drove more than fifteen miles that night before stopping between two hills on a dark rural road.

Swiftly the three worked, Codrean removing the side panels and the false floor from his car, taking out the packets of Bibles, and handing them to Luci and Gheorghe. The back seat of Gheorghe's car filled rapidly. When the last packet was stacked on the seat, he threw a pile of clothes and blankets on top.

"He asked for the confirmation form," Luci told her father.

With a gasp of dismay, Gheorghe remembered that he had left it at the apartment stuck behind the mirror in their bedroom.

The confirmation form was important to the organization that was providing the Bibles from the West. They could keep track of successful deliveries that way, and it was an encouragement to the donors to know that the Bibles were reaching their destination.

"Tell him that you will bring the form to his hotel tomorrow morning. When we return home, I will fill it out and you can deliver it on your way to school."

Codrean nodded and quickly disappeared into the night, his headlights stabbing into the darkness of the countryside.

. . . . . .

"Luci, pray!"

They had turned into their street on the way back home, their car sagging under the weight of the Bibles, when Gheorghe saw a flashlight shine through a dark, parked car. It was a signal. The secret police!

It was too late to try to turn around. That would have been a dead giveaway to anyone watching for suspicious activity. Driving slowly, his every nerve on edge, Gheorghe frantically whispered prayers.

He never got used to the tension. No matter how often he made the runs, no matter how often he transported Bibles, there were always the nervous twitches, the churning stomach, and the jangled thoughts that plagued him. But more than once the Spirit had faithfully reminded him, "My grace is sufficient for thee."

Turning off the ignition and easing out of the driver's seat, he tried not to appear ill at ease as he escorted Luci into the apartment entrance.

Lidia met them at the door and pulled them hastily inside. "Thank God, you are back!" Her face was strained in the dim hall light. "You had just left when a black car, followed by a silent ambulance, came down our street and followed you."

Her voice trembled as she spoke. "I have been praying for

you for the last two hours. The wolves are after you."

Gheorghe nodded. He sensed the truth of his wife's words. "Codrean?" Lidia asked.

"I think he is safe," Gheorghe said hopefully. "Please, Lord, don't let him get into trouble."

Both parents fell silent as they heard a sound from the living room. Luci was kneeling beside the sofa. They could hear her soft voice as she poured out her heart to God. Together, the parents joined her in fervent prayer.

"I am with you always. Don't be afraid." The words came comfortingly to Gheorghe.

Rising from his knees, he parted the curtains slightly and looked down on the street. With a muffled cry of despair, he fell to the floor. Fear gripped his heart.

Cars filled the normally empty street. The weak street lights shone on uniformed men all over the sidewalks! Clearly, there was something going on!

"Get up!"

The words came clearly to him.

"Get up. I am with you."

Gheorghe rose. "Please, Lord. I will follow your leading. Strengthen my faith. I need you!"

"I have to deliver the Bibles, Lidia! Too much money and effort has already gone into bringing these Bibles here! My small part of moving them to the next station is important to keep these Bibles going toward the Soviet Union!"

"I want to believe," Lidia's tearful words tore at Gheorghe's heart. "But I want my husband too."

"Dear Jesus," Gheorghe prayed. "This is your work, your Bibles, your venture. Help us to be brave and do our part. As you have blinded eyes before, shut the mouths of lions, and delivered many of your children, now we ask you to do the same.

"And if you choose not to do so, help us to be brave anyway. As Queen Esther said, 'If I perish, I perish.' Help us to be willing to give our lives for your sake."

"I'll go with you," Luci said quietly.

Gheorghe nodded. Lidia clasped her daughter in her arms for a brief moment. Then she let go and turned away.

The two once more descended the stairs. Taking a deep breath, Gheorghe stepped out onto the sidewalk.

There was no one there! For a moment, he could barely breathe. Fully expecting to see the same scene he had seen from his window, he could hardly grasp that now the street was empty!

His car was still parked where he had left it, sagging heavily. The back seat was still covered with the clothes and blankets they had thrown over the Bible packets. Filled with awe, the two sat in the front seats and Gheorghe started the engine. They drove slowly down the street and turned. Still, all was quiet outside.

When they reached the edge of the city, the police checkpoint was swarming with cars. That was far from normal at one o'clock in the morning. But Gheorghe was filled with the same sense of awe that had come over him when he had first stepped outside. He felt the presence of the Spirit and was not even surprised when not one of the many officers made a move to stop him.

Obviously, something else was going on. Some other kind of disturbance had taken the interest of the police that night, for Gheorghe was able to take the Bibles to the next hiding place, unload them, and return home without incident.

Chapter Seven

The Wolf Turns

"Palto, hush!" *Gabriel* said as his dog barked and leaped on the chain beside the barn door. Gabriel turned and latched the yard gate behind him. Palto gave several more yelps before sitting down on the hard-packed dirt, panting and wagging his tail.

Something was afoot. Gabriel could tell by the guard dog's tired panting. Something or someone had disturbed him.

Miriam met him at the door. "Gabriel, come in!" Her face was flushed and she pulled at his jacket. "We have visitors!"

"Who is it?"

"I don't know. Three men. Foreigners. They are in the living room. They have been here for two hours, waiting for you."

Gabriel washed his hands in the small sink beside the door. He dried them on the towel.

One thing was sure, foreigners meant Bibles. Perhaps literature too, but most importantly, Bibles.

There had been no car out on the street. Cars were few in the village; in fact, there were only three cars on this street, his and two others. Any foreign vehicle would have been obvious to himself and any other residents of the village.

Upon entering his living room, he saw the three men sitting on chairs, waiting for him. He greeted them warmly in Romanian, saying, "*Pace*" (peace), and shaking their hands in turn as they rose to their feet.

Shaking their heads, they said, "No Romanian," in their best efforts at his language.

Nodding his head, Gabriel apologetically said, "No English, no German," and they all smiled understandingly.

"Sit down," he motioned with his hand and they all sat.

One of the men drew a small black book out of his attaché case. He spoke, but of course, Gabriel could not understand.

One of the other men began holding up his fingers. Gabriel watched. Ten times he opened and closed his hands.

Had they brought a package of ten Bibles? Gabriel pointed to the Bible and motioned with his hands to indicate a package. He held up ten fingers inquiringly.

Then the first man drew a picture of a package on a slip of paper and indicated there were actually ten packages. With signs, Gabriel asked how many Bibles were in each package.

Fifty. At least numbers were written the same in English and Romanian.

Gabriel stared at the number on the paper. Five hundred Bibles! It was a big shipment. Pointing to a world map on the wall, he held up an empty palm and lifted his shoulders.

The oldest man in the group walked over to the map and pointed to Ireland. He took his finger and traced their path. They had traveled across the Irish Sea to England, across the English Channel to France, through France to Germany, south through Austria, then into Hungary, and finally across the border to Romania.

He looked at them and smiled. He could see the tiredness and the strain in their faces. Bowing his head, Gabriel let the tears flow down his face. His heart was deeply moved by these brothers who had journeyed all this way to deliver the Bibles for their brethren in the Soviet Union.

They clasped hands and prayed. Their languages were different, but they had the language of Christ in their hearts as they poured out their common needs to the Saviour.

A lone car passed outside on the street and brought Gabriel's attention to the matter of getting the Bibles out of the travelers' car. Holding an imaginary steering wheel with his hands, he lifted his eyebrows in an obvious question.

Back to the paper. The first man drew a rough map. He indicated the house they were in and then traced the main road. He drew several trees with a park bench. Next he drew a car.

Gabriel nodded in understanding. Their car was parked beside the stadium. Pointing to them and then to the drawing, he indicated that they should return to their car. Then, pointing to his watch, he indicated that he would come in his car and that they should follow him.

"Don't go anywhere by yourself. You are being followed." The warning that had come through a fellow worker at the factory surfaced in his memory.

But what could he do? These Irish brothers had come all this way with their cargo, and there was no way he could turn the Bibles away.

He clearly remembered the time two women had appeared at his door, faces drawn with anxiety. One of them had spoken a little Romanian, the other none. They had Bibles, Russian Bibles.

There had been others, foreigners, finding their way to his village close to the Ukrainian border. Sometimes they brought Romanian Bibles, but mostly they brought Russian Scriptures.

Gabriel looked through the semi-sheer curtains in the living room to the apartment building across the street. He studied a second-story window. Was a secret police agent there at his post, watching him? He had found out that a room had been rented there recently. By a spy?

Should he turn the work over to others? Perhaps there were other people in their church who could take over.

But back to the present. It was time to go.

Miriam opened the yard gate quickly as her husband drove his car out onto the street. Gabriel forced himself to not look up at that second-story window across the street. He drove in the opposite direction from which the Irish had walked earlier. He would circle around some of the back streets first.

"Lord, I know you can close the eyes of those wanting to stop your work. I trust in you. I believe in you. Please protect my Irish brothers and let them return safely to their homes. Reward them for the hours of driving and the pressure they are under. Let them feel your presence."

Gabriel spotted their car parked close to the stadium before he got there. He drove past them, never looking at their car.

He glanced in the rearview mirror and saw the car leave the parking space. Gabriel continued to pray. The first drops of rain on his window surprised him. The day had been warm and sunny with no indication of rain whatsoever, but he welcomed the shower with glee. Yes! This would make it more difficult to be followed, especially as the rain began to increase in intensity.

He glanced at the mirror again. Yes, they were still following.

Outside the village Gabriel turned left into a lot where logs were dumped; the car behind him followed. Hidden by a pile of logs, Gabriel stopped the car and jumped out into the pouring rain. He opened the trunk and turned to grab the plastic-wrapped packages of Bibles. The four worked swiftly and when the trunk was full, Gabriel piled the last four into the back seat.

Everyone was drenched, but before the three men left, Gabriel embraced them all warmly. Clasping his hands together in prayer, he said brokenly, "God go with you." His tears mingled with the rain that washed over his face. The strangers' car splashed through the mud and was gone.

Back inside his own car, Gabriel wiped his face with a towel and started his engine. The back end of his car sagged under the weight as he drove through the rain puddles. His wipers flapping furiously, he pulled out onto the road and headed directly toward his house. He met a police car going the opposite direction, but the rain was so heavy he could not see who was inside.

Then he saw the police car again, this time in his rearview mirror. They were following him! He felt apprehension creep up his spine. He felt very conscious of the sagging car. Would they suspect that he was carrying a heavy load? Or would they simply attribute it to the age of his car? All kinds of questions darted through his head. Had they seen the Irish car follow him? Had another car followed the foreigners? Sometimes the unknowns were the hardest part of the work. So many questions and so few answers!

"I place that in your care," Gabriel spoke the words into the empty car. "I put everything in your hands."

The beep of his horn brought Miriam out into the yard. He drove inside and she dutifully closed the gate behind him. Gabriel turned off the engine and opened the car door.

He could hear the police car outside on the street. He listened intently. No, they did not stop but drove on past. He was not going to be questioned this time, at least not now.

The rain had slackened and by the time he was inside and the gate was closed, the sun was already reflecting on the rain puddles. He drove the car on into his barn.

Palto came dashing out of his dog box and leaped up to greet his master. Gabriel fondled Palto's ears; then he went into the house to change into dry clothes.

.　.　.　.　.

Darkness had already come one spring evening when Gabriel heard a car slow down outside on the street. The motor stopped and someone knocked on their gate—three quick knocks and then silence.

With a smile at Miriam, Gabriel went out the back door and around to the side. The gate opened and a uniformed policeman came through the gate.

"Good evening, Gabriel," his voice was low.

"Welcome here, *Teofil*," Gabriel replied, using the officer's last name. Then he reached out and the two shook hands.

They walked around the side of the house to where no one could see them from the street. Officer Teofil said softly, "I can exchange again. Fifty."

Nodding in complete understanding, Gabriel went inside, returning with several bags that he handed to the officer. They walked together into the empty street where Teofil swiftly opened the back door of his police car and pushed a box into Gabriel's arms before hopping into the driver's seat and driving off with a friendly wave.

The box was heavy, but Gabriel's heart was light as he carried the box into the bedroom. As Miriam joined him, he carefully lifted a hardcover Bible from the box. A Romanian Bible. There were fifty of them.

Taking Miriam's hand in his own, Gabriel closed his eyes in prayer. "O God, how wonderful you are! You continue to amaze me with your ways!" On and on his prayer rose in awe and praise.

The day Officer Teofil had first approached him at work had been inauspicious enough. Gabriel had seen Teofil several times in the huge factory where he worked. At times he was the security guard at the entrance, and although the two hardly spoke to each other, they were acquainted.

"My wife is sick," Teofil had said with helplessness in his voice. "The doctor says the medicine she needs is not available in Romania unless we pay a huge sum of money. We cannot afford it.

"I know you have connections in the West." He paused and looked squarely into Gabriel's eyes. "Yes, we know you get foreign visitors from time to time." Again he let the words sink in. "Can you help me?"

Thoughts tumbled through Gabriel's mind. The police knew! For how long had they known? Why did they let him go? Were they waiting for a big haul to come and catch him red-handed?

Teofil seemed to understand his apprehensions. "Don't

worry. Even though we know, you are not in danger. You Christians are not the only ones who are dissatisfied with how things are run in our country."

To hear an officer speak what would be considered treason against the government was highly unusual.

"Please," Teofil begged.

"Write the prescription down. I will see what I can do." In spite of the real possibility that this was a sting operation, Gabriel felt the Spirit confirm in his mind that he was to do this.

It was no surprise when several months later, God provided just the medicine he had requested. From that moment on, a friendship between the Bible courier and the communist officer had developed into an amazing relationship. Gabriel was continually in awe of how God used their friendship for His glory.

"I have a report in my office that we have confiscated thirty-six Bibles from another source," Teofil told him one day. "They are Romanian hardcover Bibles. If you give me small paperback ones, you may have these, and I'll replace them with thirty-six of your less durable copies."

That had been the first of several exchanges. The pastors and leaders of the churches throughout the area prized the hardback Bibles most.

Gabriel was amazed that they had the favor of the policemen from his area. Not only were the authorities willing to ignore what they knew was going on around them, but they actually assisted the believers in different ways.

Several years later Gabriel and his wife were able to get a house because Officer Teofil helped them with legal documents. After the revolution, he did not have to go abroad to work for money to buy a house. He already had one. He was moved at how much God rewarded him and allowed him to gain favor with the local officials.

Chapter Eight

Bibles in the Beehives

The man in the wheelchair was in his mid-fifties. Sitting in the sunshine against the side of his house, he let the warm rays soak into his body. From his place under the eaves, he could see through a crack in the wooden fence in front of him and get a glimpse of what was passing by on the street of *Chilişeni.*

The village of Chilişeni was hardly different from the hundreds of other villages in northern Romania—the same cluster of houses, all fenced in with wooden fences, the same main road through the center of the village, and dirt roads leading off the main road. Storks nested on the chimney tops in the summer, their huge nests growing larger every year. People in the village gardened, herded livestock, cooked, and hung out laundry as people before them had done for generations.

This was *Bârsan's* home. Here he had lived as a boy, and perhaps because of contracting polio as a youth and ending up in a wheelchair, he came to know the comings and goings of the village folk better than anyone else.

He had married a hardworking young woman and they had two sons. It had not been an easy task to raise their boys while he was in a wheelchair, but God had been good to them. They had a comfortable, if not easy, life.

When the sound of a farm truck approaching his house became audible, Bârsan leaned forward. His faithful wheelchair squeaked under him as his weight shifted. It was not uncommon for trucks to come to the village, as huge collective farms were all around the villages. Three small taps on the horn from this particular truck were enough to send Bârsan swiftly forward, easily guiding his wheelchair over the front yard and alongside the two wide gates that led past the house to the barn.

He swung the gates open just as the truck stopped in front of him. A man in his thirties saw Bârsan and called above the noise of the motor, "Is this the place that needs honey?"

"Oh, yes," Bârsan said, and with his muscled arms swung the other gate open. The truck, loaded with beehives, entered the yard and headed toward the barn. Bârsan closed the gates, and by the time he had propelled his wheelchair around, the truck had driven into the barn.

The driver was already closing the barn doors when Bârsan reached him. Wheeling himself inside, he indicated with a wave of his hand, "Put them right there." With a nod, the driver began to work. Pulling the square wooden boxes from the truck one at a time, he placed the beehives on the dirt floor. Bârsan watched eagerly.

When the small barn door creaked open, he smiled to welcome the two men who entered. They quickly began lifting the covers from the hives and unloading packages before replacing the covers and returning the empty hives to the truck.

"Be careful with that one," the driver indicated with a nod toward the front of the truck. "There are actually bees in there."

In less than half an hour their work was finished, and with a friendly nod, the driver opened the barn doors and started his engine. Bârsan was waiting beside the gates and had them open and ready. The truck bumped out onto the road and sped away.

"Did you get a delivery?" Bârsan recognized the voice of one of the men in the village.

"Good day, John," he replied pleasantly.

"I saw that truck leave." John's voice held curiosity. "You got something delivered?"

"Oh, that was the bee truck," Bârsan explained. "You know now is the time when they take the hives to the orchards."

"Oh, yes. I'm always amazed at how they do that. It seems the bees would get really angry, being bounced around on the back of the truck like that."

A woman's voice from down the street interrupted them. "Yoo-hoo! John!"

With a small grimace, the neighbor moved on. Bârsan latched the gate and went back to the barn.

Mihai was busily passing the packages up to *Ivan* on the haymow. The two men worked swiftly, hardly pausing for a break. Bârsan counted thirty-nine packages, and in each package twenty Bibles. That would be 780 Bibles, destined for the Soviet Union.

Dry cornstalks from last year's harvest were the ideal cover for the packages. The two men spread the long scratchy stalks on top of the packages and had just jumped down from the loft when Bârsan lifted his hand to his ear and hissed, "Someone is coming!"

The two men looked around quickly and, spying a pile of potatoes in the corner, busily began sorting the potatoes.

"Bârsan!" A man's voice hailed him from outside the barn.

"In here, Samuel!"

The small door creaked open and Samuel looked in, blinking in the darkness.

"Good day! Peace!" He greeted them with the Christian greeting.

Bârsan returned the greeting as did the other two. They were all acquainted with him, as they attended church together.

"Ah, yes, time to get the potatoes in the ground," Samuel said as he saw Mihai putting wizened potatoes on a pile. He walked over and picked up one. "Even the ones you are saving seem really small. I think I would just plant them all."

"It doesn't take much for a potato to grow," Bârsan said pleasantly. "You can even plant the peelings if they are thick enough and have at least one eye."

"Well, yes," Samuel replied, and the talk turned toward gardening in general.

When he left, he had Bârsan's honing stone in his hand. "Can't think of what I did with mine. Looked all over for it this morning, but ended up working in the garden with my dull hoe. Finally I said, 'Now Samuel, you know Bârsan would be glad to let you use his until your own shows up.' So I just up and came over here.

"I will return it this evening. I don't want to lose this one and have to buy two!" With a laugh, he was gone.

Several minutes later Mihai and Ivan dusted their hands on their trousers and, with a nod, exited the barn.

"May the peace of God go with you," Bârsan said with feeling.

In the silence of the barn, Bârsan looked up at the loft. "God, I pray that you can continue to use my barn, my house, everything I have, to harbor your Word on its way north. Thank you for counting me worthy to be in your work."

He clearly remembered the scene that had started all this for him. The visitor from Denmark, who called himself Simon, had been visiting in church one Sunday morning. He knew enough Romanian to converse with the believers, and when they had gathered together for prayer, Simon had earnestly begun praying for the believers in the Soviet Union who were going through extreme hardships. Tears streaming down his face, Simon had lifted his hands toward heaven as he pled with God to somehow allow Bibles to penetrate across the border and into the hands of the desperate people there.

That was when Bârsan had prayed, "God, if you can give me any work to do, I will help. You know I cannot do much, but help me do what I can."

Soon after that a door had opened. A woman from England had visited their church. The Lord led her to Bârsan, and she had asked if he would be willing to help. No plan had been presented, no great scheme for moving Bibles; just the question, "Are you willing to help?"

How did this woman know whom to ask? How did she know he was not a secret informer who could lead her and others into danger of questioning and harassment by the police? Bârsan saw the work of the Spirit from that day on. Always he seemed to find the right people at the right place at the right time.

"Protect the many people who must be working together to do your work," he breathed. He watched the dust motes float about in the streams of sunlight that shone in through the cracks. They were seemingly without pattern, yet he knew that each mote was not unnoticed by the Creator. "You are a great God," he breathed out loud and began wheeling himself toward his house.

. . . . .

"Uncle Bârsan! The police are looking for you!" Daniel panted, his twelve-year-old eyes wide with alarm. Without waiting for a response, he darted out the yard gate and fled down the street on pounding feet.

The bee truck! It had been scheduled to arrive today. Something must have happened.

The police! Looking for him! Bârsan swallowed hard. He wet his lips with his tongue.

There had been signs. For the last months he had felt watched. Watched when he had gone to the store for bread and when he had gone to church on Sundays. Somehow, he had felt this coming.

His thoughts flying to God in a quick plea for wisdom, Bârsan waited calmly. He wheeled his chair inside and told his wife, "Maria, we might be getting visitors."

Understanding flashed across Maria's face as she picked up the water bucket and stepped outside. Returning without water, she said flatly, "They are here."

Six men in uniforms marched into their yard calling out, "Bârsan!"

"Yes?" Bârsan responded, wheeling himself to the door.

"Search the barn," the chief commanded and four of the officers headed that way.

"Sir, why? What are you doing?" Bârsan asked respectfully.

"Stolen items reported," the officer said, pushing past him and entering their house. "We will search your entire premises."

"Do you have a search warrant?" Bârsan asked quickly.

The officer completely ignored the question, but later Maria told Bârsan, "I heard him on his radio asking for a verbal search warrant."

At any time Bârsan expected to hear a triumphant shout from the barn. "Lord, blind their eyes. Not for my sake, but for the sake of those who are waiting for your Word."

"Do you know Constantine?" the chief demanded coldly of the man in the wheelchair.

"Yes, I do," Bârsan answered honestly.

"Get dressed. You must come with us."

Bârsan looked down at his paralyzed legs. "I am dressed," he said simply.

"Get another pair of trousers to take with you."

Maria caught her breath. This sounded ominous.

. . . . .

Bârsan shivered. The inside of the room was bleak and cold. Autumn nights were chilly and the open door let in cruel drafts.

"Bibles, that's what we found," the officer informed him. "Russian Bibles. Twenty-one sacks of them."

Praise God for the eighteen already are on their way to the Soviet Union! Bârsan thought gratefully.

"Why do you have Russian Bibles?"

"To give to the Russians," Bârsan said truthfully.

"And how do you plan to do that?"

"I don't know." Again, it was the truth. He didn't know. His barn was but a way station for the Word. It was obvious that the police had accomplished some major breakthrough.

"We know about your scheme to use beehives to smuggle contraband. You think you are so smart. Well," the officer smiled grimly, "you got caught because you weren't smart enough.

"That truck load of beehives was a dead giveaway. It took very few brains for the policeman to see there were no bees inside. The doors of the hives were open, and everyone knows that when you transport bees, you have to close the hives or the bees will be everywhere. Stupid people."

Bârsan felt a sinking sensation in the pit of his stomach. This indeed was a major blow.

Constantine was one of the few men involved in the Bible work whom Bârsan actually knew. There were other names he was questioned about, but for the most part, he could truthfully say he did not know them.

"Who helped you unload?"

Bârsan shook his head silently.

The blow that hit the back of his head just above the hairline was such a tremendous shock to his body that he almost lost consciousness.

"What are the names of the people who helped you unload? You are a useless cripple and you could not have done it yourself."

Bârsan thought of Mihai and Ivan, both young men with families. What would happen to them?

"I will not tell."

The next blow was expected, but there was nothing Bârsan could do to prevent it. His involuntary cry startled even himself.

"Who helped you unload?" The question was repeated, and as blow after blow kept raining on him, Bârsan felt nauseous. But before he could even think about how he felt, he was beaten again.

Always the question — "Who helped you unload?" — came dimly through his pain. How could he endure? But was this not a price he had long known he might have to pay? Was this not what he had told God he was willing to do? But there was nothing that could have prepared him for the intense pain that shot through his tortured body as his interrogators continued beating him on into the night.

At what point does the mouth no longer connect with the desire of a man's heart? When does a tortured body cry out for deliverance so greatly that the mind acquiesces? Bârsan was determined not to bend, but even as he cried to God for strength, he dimly heard himself gasp out, "Stop! It was Mihai! He helped me. And Ivan."

The beating stopped.

Something seemed to have died in Bârsan's heart. With a terrible groan, he felt himself sag defeated in his wheelchair. What had he done? Oh, God, what had he done? What would happen to his friends? To their families?

.　.　.　.　.

"Get out!"

Bârsan could hardly believe his ears. What? Get out?

The door was standing open, the officer pushing at his wheelchair. "Get out!"

He was outside! He was free?

Moaning with pain, Bârsan propelled himself through the streets toward his house. People on the sidewalks looked at him curiously, but no one spoke. News must have spread rapidly since the night before. Bârsan felt a numbness that he could not describe. His heart was heavy, his body bruised and battered, and he could hardly keep his mind rational. Now he was released and on his way home.

It was only after Maria had helped him into bed and he could gain some relief from his pain that her voice gradually penetrated his consciousness.

"… When they asked Anya why she was crying, she told them that her father had been taken to prison for having Bibles in his car. Apparently those blessed Christians from America went straight to Iaşi and filed a complaint with someone, maybe even someone in America.

"Suddenly, word spread that everyone who had been caught was to be freed! I didn't understand it, but something about President Nixon and favored nations or something. But when you came calling by the gate, I guess I was like Rhoda in Acts when Peter was released from prison. I had a hard time believing it was you! Oh, Bârsan, your head! Let me help you …"

Foreign intervention? No, divine intervention. God had used the fear of being shut off from American trade to move their government and they had released the prisoners! What about the Bibles? What would happen to them?

That is your work, Lord. It is not about me. It is not about us. It is about your Word. May the Bibles still be delivered to the hands of those searching and yearning for you. His weary brain shut off and Bârsan drifted into sleep.

Chapter Nine

A Car for God's Work

"You won a car? Because of your savings account?" *Marian* looked incredulously at his mother. "How is this possible?"

His mother laughed and handed her oldest son a paper. "Yes. I went to deposit a little more money in our savings and the clerk asked for my passport. After studying it for a while, he said I should come around to the side door to hear some good news for me. Then he told me that I had won a car. A brand new car!"

His head reeling in excitement, Marian did not understand. "But ... the government doesn't do those things! I mean, why are they giving you this car?"

"From what I understand, the state wants to encourage the citizens to save our money in their savings banks. We had very little money in September when we were first approached by the official at the post office, but your father and I decided to deposit what little we had. It was only around $500, for you know it takes most of *Tata's* wages for our living. Now here it is May and we already won a car!" The middle-aged woman shook her head in wonder.

"What will you do with it? What kind of car is it?"

Marian's mother shrugged. "I haven't thought much about it. I am not sure what kind of car it is. If I remember right, I heard something about a *Dacia*."

Marian certainly knew what he wanted to do with it—drive it! The Dacia was no Mercedes, but it was a car! What twenty-four-year-old male wouldn't want the privilege of driving a car? Cars were scarce in his part of Romania in 1979, and none of his friends or their parents even owned a car.

.   .   .   .   .

"So do you think your family was given this car just for your own use?" *Valentin* was blunt. "You think God did not have a plan when He allowed your mother to win the Dacia?"

Marian gripped the steering wheel with both hands and, looking straight ahead through the windshield, watched the long wands of the willow sway in the summer breezes.

"No, Marian, God has great plans for this car. Now that you have your driver's license and you are skillful with handling the car, I see a great door of opportunity opening up for you. Not only for you, but for many, many believers."

It was not difficult to see where this conversation was headed. "I am willing," Marian said simply.

"Your only payment will be money to cover your fuel costs. And of course you get coffee," Valentin said as he looked keenly at the young man.

"Coffee?"

Valentin nodded. "Coffee is good for staying awake when you are driving for hours and hours. Coffee is also good for gifts."

Ah, that was it. Whoever was providing the Bibles was also

sending packets of coffee along. Easy to hide and prized by many, coffee had the potential to sway some who might otherwise be reluctant to assist.

Throughout his childhood Marian had known that occasionally Bibles had become available to be passed out in their church. None of the questions he had asked his parents brought any answers. "God has provided them" was such a stock answer that Marian had no difficulty picturing the heavens open and the long arm of God reaching down to their part of Romania to give them Bibles.

As he grew older, there had been times when he wondered who was helping God. Tidbits of information gradually filtered through to him about people who were working silently and secretly to bring in the precious books.

"I need no pay," Marian said, looking at Valentin. "I will do what I can." A thrill of excitement swept over him.

Valentin saw the young man's spirit of adventure and wisely said nothing. He knew the time would come when Marian would realize that this was much more than an adventure.

.   .   .   .   .

"Time for a haircut and a shave." Valentin's mouth opened in a yawn. "*Marcu's* shop should be open by now."

Marian managed a grunt as he shifted in the driver's seat. His entire body cried out for sleep, for rest. The long, dark hours of the night seemed like a dream, and even though the morning light slightly rejuvenated him, he was still very sleepy. This cross-country trek with Valentin was his first long journey since he had agreed to "work." He had taken several short trips with Valentin, but this was the first time he had driven all night.

His companion's words finally sank into his weary brain. He looked sharply at Valentin. "Why a haircut and a shave in Sibiu?"

Stretching his arms above him in the small car, Valentin moved his shoulders stiffly. Then he pointed to a small horse pulling a loaded wagon of hay down a farm lane, remarking, "That is a big load for a small horse."

"Why do you say that?" Marian was perplexed. Maybe Valentin had not understood his question. "Why do you need …" his voice trailed away into nothing. He breathed deeply and exhaled slowly. When would he learn? How long would it take before he could refrain from voicing his curiosity and just wait to see what would develop?

"There will be lots of things you will want to know," Valentin had told him when they had first started working together. "The best thing is to follow your instructions without asking questions. The success of our work lies in not knowing too much. Someday you will understand the wisdom of this."

Now he had failed again. Valentin had reminded him by making a statement totally irrelevant to his question. He had changed the subject.

Marian agreed meekly, "That is a rather small horse."

Suddenly Valentin began to laugh. He slapped Marian on the knee. "Don't worry, son. God is taking you through His school, and you are doing well." Then in a more serious tone he added, "But there is not much room for mistakes. Our work is too serious, and we have many people depending on each part of the mission. May God help us."

Their entry into Sibiu took them through the streets of the city and on into the center. When they reached the downtown area, Valentin told Marian to pull over and park the car. "Bring all your personal belongings with you, including the registration. Give me the keys and registration." This time Marian did not ask any questions. He picked up his overnight bag and handed the keys and registration card to his friend before they got out.

Marcu barely nodded as the two men entered the barber shop. He continued cutting his customer's hair. Valentin slipped off his coat and hung it on a hook beside a curtained doorway. Then he and Marian settled themselves into empty chairs.

While they waited for Marcu to finish with his customer, Marian began nodding as he dozed. It felt good to be out of the car and finally able to take a nap.

At last the customer rose from his chair and paid Marcu. Valentin got up and took the empty chair. Marian could hear the two talking. It was just ordinary conversation about the economy and how their families were doing. Then sleep overcame him and he dozed, hardly aware of where he was. He dimly realized that customers occasionally entered and left the shop.

He woke with a start when his companion nudged him. "Do you want a shave?"

Rubbing his eyes, he glanced at Valentin. He shrugged his shoulders and said sleepily, "Do I need one?"

Valentin nodded. "You could use one."

During his shave he was vaguely aware of movement in the back room of the barbershop, and the curtain in the doorway swayed silently as though someone had stepped close to it.

Valentin's jacket stirred ever so slightly on its hook.

Then the shave was done and Marian stood up. Valentin paid the barber, took his coat, and the two returned to the parked car.

"Do you remember the way back home?" Valentin asked when they were settled inside.

"Home?" Marian asked quizzically.

"Yes," Valentin smiled. "Seven hours and we should be back in our homes."

Dutifully, Marian steered the Dacia into the traffic and re-traced the route of the morning drive. His brain was reeling. Where was the meeting point? Would it be on the way back? Why had they spent so much time at the barber shop? When would they get the Bibles?

He was glad when they got out of the city and back on the highway. He picked up speed. Something in the car's handling felt different. He turned the steering wheel slightly, and the car swayed rather sluggishly. It felt as though there was something in the trunk. Something heavy.

Marian had to grin to himself. Okay, the pieces of the puzzle were beginning to fit together. The barber shop had only been a place for someone to come, get the keys from Valentin's coat pocket, take the car to some secret location, load the trunk with Bibles, bring the car back, park it, and return the keys.

Had the car been parked in the same spot where he had left it? Marian tried to remember. He hadn't paid attention. It didn't really matter, he thought, but reminded himself to be more observant next time.

Marian turned toward Valentin, intending to ask for the registration papers, but before he could form the request, Valentin was handing them to him. "You pass," the older man said quietly. "God has blessed you with the ability to think, and I know He will use you mightily in His work."

There was no need for words between the two. Marian realized that communication did not depend on words alone. In this work it was important to allow others to do their work without questions.

· · · · ·

It had been only two days since Marian and Valentin had returned from their trip to Sibiu. They had unloaded the packages in the basement of their church where the little children met for Sunday school. That big desk in the middle of the room was more than a table; it was a hollow cube with ample space inside.

Now Marian was alone. He had gone to the church at eleven o'clock that night, had taken two packages as instructed, and had put them into the trunk of the car.

"Someone will meet you at the entrance of the construction site," Valentin had told him. So when he pulled up at the gates, he was prepared when someone suddenly appeared out of the darkness, opened the passenger side door, and sat inside.

"Go," was the only word spoken.

Marian steered the car straight ahead until a guard flashed a light at him. Marian knew this meant he was to stop. He rolled down his window.

The guard shone his light inside onto Marian's face and next onto his companion. Straightening up, he wordlessly motioned to Marian to move forward.

They drove into the construction site. Following his companion's directions, Marian steered the car toward a backhoe.

"Give me the key," his companion requested as they stopped. Hopping out, he went back to the trunk. Marian watched in fascination as he saw the two packages disappearing into the darkness of the backhoe bucket. The stranger handed him the keys again.

"Go back out."

They drove back to the gates where the guard motioned them through. The unknown companion said, "Stop." The passenger door opened, and the man disappeared into the night almost before Marian managed to stop the car.

Driving back home, Marian began praying that the Bibles would reach their destination and also praying for the many other people who were involved in the work. He knew he had only a fragment of information and marveled at how God was using so many people to work together in order to get His printed Word to the hungry and desperate believers.

Chapter Ten

Bibles Know No Borders

The construction site covered as much as ten acres. Cumbersome bulldozers, their blades apparently making little progress, pushed dirt into enormous piles. Then they backed up to take another layer of dirt off the dam floor. Gigantic cranes, their buckets grabbing at the dirt and then swinging dexterously in spite of their size, moved in synchronized movements, almost graceful in the regularity of the pivoting long necks, like giraffes grazing on a brown landscape.

Dump trucks scuttling back and forth provided yet another dimension of movement to the project. They dumped their loaded beds onto what was to be the banks of the huge dam, where yet more bulldozers smoothed out the dirt and packed it well.

The dam site was situated right on the border of Romania and the Soviet republic of Ukraine. To the east and west of the project were the usual border fences with their electronic means of keeping each country's citizens safe from foreign enemies, as the governments wanted the people to believe.

It was complicated to accomplish any project involving neighboring countries, even supposedly friendly ones, and this project had been no exception. Countless hours must have been spent in the planning and engineering stages, but the workers had only been too happy to begin. At least they would have steady work for a long time.

For Daniel, the job had indeed been welcome. Outgoing, ready to tackle almost any job, he had never been idle. Give him a job to do anytime and he was right at it. Hearty, easy to get along with, and ready to share a good story with a laugh, Daniel had been glad when the project got underway.

As a crane operator, Daniel had a lot of time to observe the activities around him. His quick mind had soon traced the predictable routes of the dump trucks, bulldozers, and cranes. He had even found a pattern followed by the security officers who patrolled the international site. Although the officers didn't exactly follow the same protocol every day, Daniel still saw a regularity in their carefully calculated efforts to keep everyone on guard.

Although no one spoke openly about it, most of the workers were keenly aware of the great potential that being on this project offered. Taking contraband—such as drugs, alcohol, or cigarettes—from Romania into Ukraine could be extremely lucrative for any successful smugglers. Another contraband item not allowed into Ukraine was propaganda, and Daniel knew Bibles were considered propaganda.

With practiced eyes he watched as the dump trucks drove north out of Romania with their loads of gravel, imported to provide mass to the earthen dam. When God created the world, he saw to it that Romania had the gravel needed by the Soviet Union at such a time as this.

Occasionally he would watch "certain trucks" come down

the earthen track toward him. He would direct the drivers with hand signals to dump their loads of gravel beside a gigantic pile of culverts. This gravel pile was a reserve for them to use when the trucks weren't running. Most of the time Daniel didn't get out of his crane cab to direct those drivers. He was too busy scooping up the fill by the bucketfuls and loading the trucks as they rumbled up to be filled.

The early morning hours were the times Daniel usually enjoyed the best. In the middle of the summer, even though the sun was over the horizon by five o'clock, the air was cool and there was a vibrancy in the air that he enjoyed. In his exuberant way Daniel would look for a chance to leap out of the cab after a truck was loaded and run up to the top of the pile of culverts. Stretching his arms upward, he would take deep breaths before turning around and leaping down again. Sometimes he would bend low and run through the culverts until the sound of a truck engine sent him dashing back to his crane.

This pattern continued for months. It took a long time to laboriously scrape the soil away and haul it off to make the water reservoir the hydroelectric plant would need. The dam was slowly being constructed, though even a casual observer could see that it would take years to complete.

·　·　·　·　·

One morning just after a truck had dumped a load of gravel on the reserve pile, Daniel jumped out of the cab of the crane he was operating. Without turning his head, his eyes cased the area. Then, as was usual, he went around the gravel pile and grabbed a dusty canvas bag at its base before disappearing inside a culvert pipe.

The air was still outside, the hum of the departing truck growing fainter and fainter. At the other end of the pipe Daniel turned the corner and pushed the canvas bag into a cavity between the round culverts. Then he straightened up, dusted his hands off, and ran up to the top of the pipes as usual.

There was an alertness about his attitude as he stood up on top of the pile, surveying the construction site. At the same time his face wore a look of peaceful satisfaction, as though he felt fulfilled in the work he was doing.

The sound of an approaching truck sent him bounding down off the pile of pipes, and with a cheerful wave to the driver, he revved up his idling engine and filled the waiting dump bed.

Several days later a motorcycle sputtered to a stop close to where Daniel was working. The sidecar attached to the motorcycle did not have the usual seat for an extra passenger, but was stripped to provide extra cargo space.

Daniel seemed oblivious as the Ukrainian man, *Yuri*, stopped the motorcycle and walked behind the culvert pile. He reappeared a moment later with a bag that looked much like one of the sacks of concrete he typically transported, though it seemed lighter.

Two more bags and the sidecar was loaded. Yuri left without as much as a glance at Daniel, who continued his work and ignored the motorcycle heading north into Ukraine.

Daniel's secret work had all begun one day several months earlier. He had been waiting in the crane cab for yet another dump truck to fill. As was his custom, he pulled his treasured Romanian Bible from his carry bag, opened it, and began reading. He had heard that Bibles were scarce and difficult to obtain in the Soviet Union. In his native Romania it was not too difficult to get a personal Bible, yet there was a shortage, so when someone had a Bible, it was well taken care of and cherished.

The knock on the window of his cab startled him. Outside, the grinning face of the Ukrainian driver looked through the glass.

"Ready for the load," he yelled in Romanian.

Because of the shifting border between Romania and Ukraine, the Ukrainians in the southern part of their country spoke Romanian fluently. And since Russian was a required language course in Romania, Daniel's Russian was quite good. Naturally, this helped greatly as the two countries collaborated on the dam project.

Just as the driver prepared to step off the crane, his eyes dropped to the Bible in Daniel's lap. He froze.

Daniel had closed the Bible and was putting it back in his bag. When he saw the driver's eyes fastened on the black book, his hand stopped in midair.

The driver swung himself around to the open window. "What is that?"

"It's a Bible," Daniel said simply.

"A Bible?" The driver's voice sounded hoarse even above the idling engine.

Daniel nodded.

"May I see it?" An eager hand reached toward the book.

Daniel handed it to the man.

There was a reverence as the rough, work-hardened hand took the Bible and gently pressed it to his chest. Shutting his eyes tightly, the driver took his free hand and raised it toward heaven. A stream of praise and thanksgiving in Russian rose from the weeping man's heart. The air was charged with holy energy, and Daniel felt God's presence strongly as the rejoicing man prayed, his words flowing like living water out of some deep place inside.

As though he suddenly remembered where he was, the Ukrainian driver looked around hastily and, addressing Daniel, said, "This is the first time I have ever held a Bible! Can you believe it? Here, at work, God has allowed me to hold His book!"

As though some magnet drew him, he carefully opened the Bible and began to read aloud from John 1. "In the beginning was the Word, and the Word was with God, and the Word was God." He read the words in Romanian and then translated them into Russian. Lifting his eyes to Daniel, he begged with tears, "Please give me this Bible! I will pay you for it!" Then in desperate tones he almost babbled, "Please, sell me this Bible. I will give you … I will give you my whole month's wages for it! Please!"

Daniel heard the desperation. He knew this man was willing to make a great sacrifice in order to persuade him to sell the Bible. In Ukraine a month's wages were not very much, yet greatly needed in every household. Starvation was never far from most of the workers' lives.

Daniel looked down at the open book. He saw where he had underlined several favorite verses. "This is my personal Bible. I think I can get you another one. I'll bring it here, and the next time you come I will give it to you."

Shaking his head determinedly, the driver said, "No, I will keep this one until you come with another one. Then I will give this one back." Although he said it in a rather teasing manner, Daniel knew it was no light matter. Stark hunger stared right out of the man's soul.

"Okay," Daniel laughed, and as the driver dropped onto the ground hugging his precious gift, he began loading the truck.

He never saw that driver again.

At least Daniel never saw him again face to face. Many times when he closed his eyes to pray, the Ukrainian driver's face would come to him. Over and over again he saw the tears of joy streaming down his cheeks. He saw the hunger in his eyes as the driver hugged the Bible to his chest. His voice, too, kept coming to Daniel. "Is that a Bible? I have never touched a Bible before!"

Finally Daniel cried out, "Okay, God, I am willing. I will do whatever I can to help take your Word to the desperately hungry in Ukraine. Surely you have given me this job for a reason. It was a divine appointment that led that driver to me on that specific day, just at the moment when I was reading the Bible.

"I know there is a cost involved, God. I know some of your children have suffered arrests, beatings, imprisonments, and, yes, even death because of being caught smuggling Bibles. But I cannot refuse you. You gave heaven's best when you gave us Jesus. Your Father heart was touched deeply when you saw your Son on the cross for my sins. Helping your children get your Word is the least I can do."

It had not been easy. Just finding the Bibles had been a challenge.

Discreetly mentioning the need to brothers he trusted, Daniel knew better than to openly inform anyone of what he was doing.

God provided in ways that Daniel knew very little about.

"A gift is in your woodshed" meant that Bibles had somehow materialized. How they had gotten there was not something to be investigated. To know that God had provided was enough. If they were Russian Bibles, Daniel would package them to resemble bags of concrete. If Romanian, he would leave them in churches.

Even after getting past the first hurdle of obtaining Bibles, Daniel was faced with the task of getting them into the construction site. There was security control even for the Romanians getting onto the job.

God had opened the door, and Daniel had been instrumental in gaining the confidence of a crane operator at the gravel quarry. Several bags of Bibles placed in the crane bucket at night were covered with gravel, and the next morning the first bucket load of gravel that cascaded into the empty truck contained the packets of Bibles. Not many, just several or one at a time, and only on certain trucks. This provided a way of getting them inside the project.

That is where Daniel's actual work began. Moving the Bibles into a safe hiding place was his main responsibility. He was but a link in the chain that moved the Bibles toward their destination.

Yuri was the next link. As the driver of the motorcycle, he would pick up three bags of concrete at a time and chug away into Ukraine. Why it was that concrete was taken across the border this way, Daniel never knew. He just saw an opportunity and was willing to use it.

Daniel had felt sure the Holy Spirit had prompted him to approach the sober, silent Yuri.

"I need you to help me," Daniel had said one day.

Yuri had placed the first bag of concrete into the sidecar. He had only briefly glanced at Daniel when he had been addressed. "What is in it for me?" Typical of people brought up under repression, Yuri went right to the heart of the matter.

"The satisfaction of providing your people with books," Daniel replied truthfully.

Silently Yuri had stacked the next two bags of concrete into the sidecar. Then with a glance at Daniel and a brief shrug, he had left.

"There is a bag between the third and fourth pipes," Daniel told him the next day. "Put the bag into the tool house beside the mechanic's garage."

Daniel had never seen the tool house. He had only been given those instructions and he had memorized them. Would Yuri comply? Would someone on the other side be led into a trap? Daniel prayed fervently in his spirit.

Yuri did not acknowledge his instructions, but Daniel saw him disappear around the side of the pile of culverts. Soon he reappeared with his bag of Bibles! Daniel felt thanksgiving wash over him as he turned to load the next truck. He had not realized how nervous he was until he saw his knuckles, white and tightly gripping the controls.

Did Yuri ever know what he was transporting? Did he ever look? What would be his reaction if he were caught? Daniel would never know the answers to those questions. He just knew that for the next three and a half years, Yuri would check for packages. If there were any there, he would place them into his sidecar and head north across the border.

* * * * *

"Good morning," Daniel greeted the security control one morning. "It's getting colder every day."

The officer merely nodded. His eyes searched the inside of Daniel's car.

Daniel shrugged his neck deeper into his heavy jacket. He clapped his hands together. Would this be a morning when the guard decided to search his car? Or would he wave him on through? Daniel knew there was no established pattern. They might search thoroughly one day and hardly glance at him the next.

"Get out," the officer's voice broke through his thoughts.

Obediently Daniel opened the door and got out. He stepped to one side.

The officer knelt on the front seat and felt underneath with his gloved hand. He patted the seat backs and opened the glove compartment. "Open your bag," he commanded, indicating Daniel's carry bag.

Daniel reached into the back of the car and opened the bag. His lunch was inside, along with his small Bible.

"I don't know why you waste your time taking that book with you all the time," the officer snorted.

"I take the Word of God with me wherever I go," Daniel said cheerfully. He crossed his arms in front of his bulky coat.

There was no reply. The guards had seen Daniel's Bible many times before.

With a stiff nod the officer left, and Daniel settled himself in the driver's seat again. Singing at the top of his voice, Daniel opened his coat as he drove toward the construction site. He began pulling small paper-backed New Testaments from under his shirt until there were five of them on the seat beside him.

"You not only shut the lions' mouths for that Daniel, but also kept the lion away from this Daniel. Thank you, Jesus!" Five more precious books to be wrapped up and shipped into Ukraine.

Over and over in Daniel's mind he played out scenes of eager believers reacting with joy and amazement as Bibles were placed into their hands. He envisioned old people, lonely and unable to work, reaching out for the Word of God and, with tears, thanking their Lord. He saw pastors, laboring carefully with handwritten copies, being moved deeply as Bibles were provided. And young believers, new in their faith, having their trust in God strengthened as a Bible from the West was placed into their eager hands.

Chapter Eleven

Packaged in Paint Cans

"Lord Jesus, we pray for healing for Brother *Victor*. As you have healed in the past, so we look to you for healing now."

The believers who gathered in *Emil's* house were clustered around Victor. Several had placed their hands on the sick man's body. The pastor, *Gigi*, had anointed Victor's head with oil, and now they prayed together for the young man's headache to be relieved in the name of Jesus.

"My headaches are becoming increasingly severe and frequent," Victor had told Emil that day. "I don't know if I can continue working if I don't get relief."

"Come to my house tonight," Emil had urged. "I will call for some of the believers to come and we will pray. God can heal you. He has healed others and He can heal you."

"I don't know if I have enough faith," Victor had protested. "But I want to believe."

Emil once more pressed him. "Come to my house. We don't have time to talk any more right now, but we can pray together tonight."

Eleven of them came. Eleven men and women who believed in the healing power of the Lord Jesus Christ came to pray to the Great Physician for healing.

"I feel hot," Victor said now, as those who were praying paused. "Something is sweeping all over my body."

"Yes, Jesus, thank you," Emil raised his hands and prayed.

"Whew!" Victor wiped his forehead. "Something is happening."

The home was one in a row of simple, rough village houses that lined the street. Emil's house was hardly any different from the rest, enclosed with the usual head-high wooden fence forming a U shape and an open shed connecting the house to the barn. That night the glory of the Lord visited the handful of believers as they prayed and worshiped. The humble dwelling was transfigured into a holy place when the Spirit of the Lord came and brought healing to the suffering young man.

"Tell Victor about the time the Lord brought healing into your family," the pastor urged Emil as they got up from their knees. "I think your testimony would encourage him."

Victor was still breathing deeply, a look of wonder in his eyes. Facing his host he asked, "What is your story?"

Emil looked at the wooden floor boards for a moment. With a slight smile he began.

"I had been a Christian for only a year when I sensed that God was calling me to a deeper walk with Him. I felt my faith was too weak, and yet something inside me kept calling me to surrender everything to the Lord.

"We had our first two children by then. My wife and I were both going to church, and even though on the outside it may have looked as though we were faithful believers, I still had not yielded myself totally to Christ."

The room quieted as Emil continued his story. Several had

heard it before, but they enjoyed listening to the testimony once again. *Sara* brought in hot water and made tea for everyone. She looked at her husband as he closed his eyes in prayer for a moment.

"*Daniela* was four years old, and we had just gotten a report from the doctor that she was having severe kidney problems. On top of that, our two-year-old son, Daniel, had still not spoken a word. He only grunted and made signs, and although we had him checked, the doctor said there was nothing wrong with him. But we sensed that something was holding back his speech, and we often prayed for our children.

"One night I felt that God was speaking to me directly. There was something He wanted me to be willing to do." Glancing out at the dark autumn night, Emil got up and pulled the curtains together more tightly.

Heads nodded. All of them were involved now. They knew the work God had called Emil to do.

Victor listened intently. He had only recently been invited to help with loading and unloading Bibles as they traveled through this part of Romania.

"As God was dealing with my heart, I felt a great pressure on me. My daughter was sick, my son was mute, and now there was something else God was asking me to do. I faced a great struggle. I knew what the consequences could be if I joined the work. I knew what happened to others.

"But the weight did not leave. So I called for Gigi to come." Emil paused and looked gratefully at their pastor. "I told him what was happening."

Sara dabbed the corner of her eyes. Just hearing the story was bringing back memories.

"To my surprise, Gigi did not encourage me to do anything. 'We will pray for your children,' was what he said when I had finished talking.

"As he began to pray for Daniela, something happened inside me. I felt lighter, as though some load had lifted from my heart. Then he prayed for Daniel and finally he prayed for me."

By this time tears were running freely down Emil's cheeks, and more than one person's eyes were wet.

"Oh, I praise God for the release I felt in my soul! He is so good!" Emil once more paused, taking a deep breath before continuing. "I found myself not only willing to join the work, but I actually felt a joy I can't express. We felt the presence of God with us."

"Glory to Jesus," Gigi said, lifting his hands toward the ceiling. "It is all because of you, God."

There was a murmur of assent and more than one was praying softly as they listened to their brother's testimony.

"I think it was an hour later when I asked Daniel if he wanted a drink before he went to bed, and for the first time in his life, he spoke! He said 'Yes' so distinctly!

"I remember the room was very quiet. Gigi was still there.

"I asked my son, 'What is your name?' and the answer came right back. He said 'Daniel' very clearly. From that moment on he spoke. Something was loosened inside him, and he began speaking just like a normal two-year-old.

"And another marvelous thing happened. A month later when we took Daniela to the doctor, he checked her and told us that her kidney problem had vanished. It was totally gone!"

"Just like my headache," Victor interjected with a smile. "Oh, truly the Lord is wonderful! How I thank Him!"

A feeling of awe and wonder swept over them. Lifting their hands in prayer, the group began to worship and pray once more. Emil's heart swelled within him. He felt the power of the Spirit within him, and he wept as he praised His Lord.

A flashlight shone suddenly through the curtained window directly onto Emil's face.

The police! They had come to search his house!

"Police!" Emil hissed to Gigi.

Immediately, Gigi took charge. "Keep praying," he said to the believers. "Keep right on praying."

Emil motioned slightly with his head toward the bedroom, and two men slipped quietly into the room and closed the door.

When the front door was kicked open, the praying voices wavered slightly but continued.

"Emil *Andrieş*!" the commanding voice of the officer called out above the voices.

Emil went toward the door, threading his way among the standing and kneeling figures in his living room.

"Yes, sir," he said quietly and politely.

"We have a search warrant." Turning his head slightly, he ordered the two officers with him, "Search!"

Taking a sweeping glance at the group in the living room, the officers hesitated.

"Everyone leave. You have no permission to have a gathering. What is this? A birthday party or something? Where is the cake?"

Nobody answered him directly. Several of the women began clearing the cups and assisting Sara.

"I said 'Get out!' " The officer was getting frustrated. "Search the kitchen," he directed the other two officers.

Emil forced himself to breathe slowly and evenly. As the officers went into the kitchen, several of the men began exiting the house, brushing past the official still surveying the room.

Gigi was gone. He had disappeared out the back door right after the front door had been kicked open. It was better for him and the others if he was not recognized.

Although the kitchen was not large, the officers searched diligently. Opening every cupboard door, pulling out the cooking pots and leaving them on the floor, thumping on the walls with the ends of their nightsticks, they continued to search. It took several minutes for them to push open the trapdoor overhead. One stood on a chair and flashed his light around the attic.

As the believers left one by one, Emil and Sara stood side by side as the officers continued to ransack their house. Thankfully, the children had all gone to their grandparents' house for the evening and were spared the fright.

"Search the bedrooms," the officer directed, crossing the now almost empty living room and kicking open the wooden door.

From where Emil stood, he could see straight into the bedroom, and as the officers searched with their flashlights, he swallowed hard. Their bed stood in the middle of the room as always. Against the wall, Sara had stacked boxes to store their winter clothes in. Their closet was partially visible beside the window.

The window faced the street outside. Though heavily curtained, it was always quite easy to hear traffic and voices from the street; only a few feet separated the house from the road. The wooden fence was hardly twelve inches away from the glass.

The boxes were unceremoniously pulled away from the wall and the contents dumped on the floor. Tramping over the spilled contents, the officers opened the wardrobe doors, and pushing the clothes aside, they searched the corners without regard to the mess they were making.

It was with relief that Emil watched them leave their bedroom and search the two small rooms where the children slept. Once more, everything was turned upside down in their search.

"Search the barn."

Two officers left while the head official kept watch in the house, his eyes stern and unflinching. "One of these days, we'll catch you." The words were flung at Emil as the officers left at the end of their fruitless, two-hour search. "We know what you are up to."

Emil said nothing.

He was helping the weeping Sara when the children came home. They needed no words of explanation. Even in their young years they knew a lot about life under the repressive regime. They had learned early on not to ask questions.

. . . . .

Prying the lid off a big paint can, Emil carefully placed the lid on the table top. Then carefully tipping the heavy can, he poured the white paint into a tin bucket until almost half the paint was out. He set the can on the floor.

Victor slipped a plastic-wrapped package right into the paint remaining in the can. The heavy package sank to the bottom and Emil poured the paint back into the can until it was filled up to the brim once more.

He opened another can. Again he poured half of the paint into the bucket. Victor inserted a package and refilled the can with paint. This process was repeated until twelve cans of white paint, each with an inserted package, stood on the floor. The lids were tightly clamped back on, and all spills were wiped from the floor of this room under the garage.

The two men hauled the cans up the narrow stairway. They replaced the boards in the garage floor, stacked the rough-cut lumber on top of the opening, and sat down on top of the cans. They did not speak. They just sat there, waiting.

"You need to stop." The words reverberated in Emil's brain. He could still hear Gigi's words clearly. He had said that the Sunday after the police had searched their house. "That was too close. We cannot endanger the work."

Emil had nodded, knowing that his pastor's words were true. He was being watched. He had sensed it before. Going to work, coming home from work, going to the store; in fact, almost every time he had gone outside recently, he would see a police officer in plain clothes. So this was to be his last night, at least for awhile. He would have to let others continue.

As he waited beside Victor, Emil's thoughts flew back to the prayer meeting at his house when they had prayed for Victor to be healed. "Are your headaches still gone?" he whispered to his companion.

Victor looked at him with shining eyes. He nodded his head and raised his hands exultantly over his head. He grasped Emil's hand firmly and pressed it against his chest.

That had been quite the night. The wonderful gift of healing given to Victor greatly overshadowed the police visit that followed, especially because the Bibles had been removed so quickly and the searchers had found no trace of what had been stored in their bedroom.

Surely it had been God who had given the two men the ability to quickly and quietly shuttle the ten boxes of Bibles out from under their bed and through the window before the police had searched their bedrooms. Surely it had been God who had made the officers search the kitchen and the attic before the bedroom. Surely it had been God who had used the shuffle and scuffle of the believers' feet to muffle any sound that might have penetrated the closed doors. The removal of the incriminating Bibles had been completed before that room was even entered by the officers!

Even now, Emil marveled at the speed and precision with which the underground method of moving Bibles worked. He was convinced that God was the mastermind of the entire route. And he only knew this portion of the route!

The sound of a motor outside the garage broke into Emil's reverie. Both men stood up and waited. As the sound of the engine neared, they got ready. They swung the garage doors open swiftly and the vehicle drove inside.

The garage doors were shut and the driver's door of the van opened. A woman stepped out. With only a nod toward the men, she opened the back doors of the van and hopped inside. When they placed the heavy paint cans on the floor of the van, she pushed them forward and arranged them against the back of the driver's seat.

It took only a few minutes before the cans were loaded, the doors closed again, and the van backed out. The woman was on her way. Emil gave Victor a brief hug in the darkness and walked quickly toward home. With his ears tuned to the night world around him, he pictured the van's journey northward. North toward the Soviet border.

He thought about the driver. The number of times he had met her had given him no insight into her character. In fact, they hardly ever spoke to each other, and he did not even know her name. In his mind he called her "Paint Lady."

For some reason she came into Romania to buy paint or sometimes detergent in bulk and took her cargo north into the Soviet Union. Walking through the darkness, Emil began to imagine how it must be for the woman to approach the border, knowing that she was carrying concealed Bibles. Did her heart begin to beat harder as the Romanian officials inspected her van? Did her heart pound even quicker when the Soviet authorities did their inspection? Or were there people there at the border who knew what she was doing and were actually helping her?

As a matter of fact, Emil did not even know if the woman was a believer or not. He did not know whether she was being paid to take Bibles across the border and into the eager hands of the Christians there, or whether she was doing it voluntarily. One thing he sensed though: God was doing this. There were too many people involved, too many things that could go wrong, and yet thousands of Bibles were being brought into his country and successfully transported on into the Soviet Union. To be sure, there were arrests. There were people imprisoned when caught, and there were even "accidents" that took the lives of believers, and yet the work went on.

As he neared his home, he felt a certain sadness settle over him. He would have to quit. The search party that had ransacked his house had shown him that. He was being watched.

Yet he felt the blessing of God on his life and on his efforts. Even though he did not feel he was doing much compared to what he longed to do, he felt humbled that he had been able to assist in God's work of getting Bibles into the hands of those who hungered and thirsted after God.

As his mind traveled back to the prayer meeting in his house, he rejoiced. "That's what it's all about," he whispered to himself. "It's all about you, Jesus."

It was about people praying. It was about worshiping Jesus. It was about the sick being healed. It was about sinners repenting and turning their lives over to the Lord. That was the Gospel at work, right among them in their own lives.

"I refrained from the Bible work for four years," Emil told us. "Then God opened the doors for me to help again. By that time, I was no longer being followed."

He estimates that over 4,000 Russian Bibles and New Testaments went through his way station close to Gherla, besides the innumerable Romanian Bibles that stayed in their area and were freely distributed among the believers.

Chapter Twelve

Across the Border in Bread and Honey

"I'm going to visit my uncle in *Cernăuți*," *Ilie* informed the border patrol when asked to state his purpose for visiting the Soviet Union. Wisps of snow blew between the inspection booth and the boy on his motorcycle.

"How long?"

"Three days."

"What is in there?" The officer pointed to his sidecar.

"Bread and honey," Ilie answered simply.

It was not unusual for Romanians heading north to take food with them. People in the Soviet Union were hard pressed for food most of the time, but especially in winter.

The officer nodded his head toward the rubber cover of the sidecar, and Ilie removed the straps and pulled back the tarp. Loaves of bread nestled alongside several jars of honey. Taking a loaf, Ilie laid it on the counter of the guard booth. "Take one. My mother bakes good bread." He slid a small jar of honey across too.

The officer frowned but did not refuse the food. "Why are you not in school?" the Russian patrol asked, looking at Ilie's passport and noting that this young boy was only seventeen.

Ilie's answer was somewhat muffled by the heavy wool scarf he had wrapped around his neck. A gust of wind blew bits of hard snow into their faces. With a quick stamp, the official granted Ilie a visa and waved him through before closing the window and retreating to the relative warmth of his booth.

The sidecar jounced alongside his cycle, the tarp once more fastened securely. Ilie felt a surge of excitement course through him. He had crossed the border!

This was not his first visit inside the Soviet Union. It was not necessarily easy to cross the border from Romania, yet it was fairly common for the two countries to see quite a bit of travel, especially since the southern part of the Soviet Union had belonged to Romania at one time and many people had relatives in each country. But this was his first trip taking bread across. Especially Bread with a capital B!

"These are the loaves for you to give away," his mother had told him as he had helped her pack the sidecar. "You will remember which ones are safe, right?"

"Yes, Mother. I don't want to give the wrong ones."

"This is the loaf for you to eat on the road," his mother had told him. "Just don't eat too much until you are on the other side of the border." She looked at her son with intensity. "My mother heart doesn't want you to do this, but God tells me it is okay. I choose to trust Him and not my feelings."

Inside most of the loaves, precious gifts had been enclosed in moisture-proof packages and baked. At first they had experimented with handfuls of paper, and when they had succeeded in baking the paper without damaging it, they had carefully inserted Russian New Testaments. The loaves looked just like any other loaves when they were pulled from the oven. Putting small New Testaments inside little jars and placing them inside the larger containers filled with honey was somewhat easier, but perhaps more risky.

As Ilie traveled across the frozen landscape toward his uncle's house, he felt a warm glow surround his heart. He felt privileged to have been trusted by those who were involved in taking Bibles across the border. He knew that his young age might have been a concern for some, but he also knew that it was a good cover for what he was doing. Many university students traveled over school holidays.

"O God, thank you for all this bread! And honey too!" Ilie's aunt exclaimed gratefully as Ilie carried armloads of food inside the apartment.

"Please wait until I have it all in," Ilie cautioned. "There is some for now and some for later."

His aunt nodded and held the door open for him. "I'll wait."

After the last load was safely inside, Ilie asked, "May I please have a sharp knife?"

Taking a loaf of bread, he cut partly into the middle of the loaf, turning the bread so the cut went all the way around the bread, but not slicing into the center. Then, breaking the loaf in half, he exposed the package, unwrapped it, and gave it to his aunt.

"*Novea Zavet!*" (New Testament) his aunt breathed quietly and turned the pages. "It was baked inside the bread!" She looked inquiringly at the other loaves piled on the table.

Ilie nodded and again cut into a loaf. He placed the package on the table and reached for the third loaf.

"Let me help," his aunt said, reaching for a loaf.

"Not that one," Ilie said, selecting a different one. "Some are just bread and others contain the Bread of Life."

Twenty-four loaves of bread were cut apart and the packages removed. The table was littered with bread crumbs, and the three whole loaves remaining were placed to one side.

"I need to hide these Testaments," Aunt Elena told him.

"Wait," Ilie grinned, "there is more."

"But I thought you said those loaves don't have any…" Her voice trailed away as she watched Ilie reach for a jar of honey.

"I need to pour some honey out into a pan," Ilie said. "There is something sweeter than honey inside."

Aunt Elena understood immediately. She shook her head in amazement as Ilie extracted a sticky jar from inside the container and set it into another empty pan. The honey was cold and stiff and barely flowed, but it would clean up nicely after it warmed up.

"Which jars?"

Ilie set five jars on the table. Two more jars remained on the floor.

The twenty-nine New Testaments were packed into a box, and Aunt Elena disappeared into her bedroom. What good news she had to tell Vladimir tonight!

. . . . .

Snow drifts still lay alongside the train tracks, although warmer weather promised spring days were really here. There was still a faint light in the west, and the night wind was starting to bite again. The railway station had the usual passengers waiting for the next train, their suitcases by their side, and their backs turned against the wind.

Ilie waited on the motorcycle seat behind a Russian brother.

Another cycle with a driver waited alongside them. Both cycles had the common sidecars attached to them.

The whistle of an approaching train came through the evening air. Ilie felt the familiar twinge inside his chest. No longer was he taking occasional trips into the Soviet Union, hiding only a few Bibles at a time. That first trip had been over ten years ago, and the first of many, but now he did not carry Bibles across the border. After marrying Maria, he began to coordinate the pick-ups inside the Soviet Union.

The train could now be seen coming down the tracks, its whistle blowing for a stop. It was a Soviet engine, pulling the passenger train from Romania.

Although they were parked across the tracks from the railway station, they could see the usual policemen on the platform outside the station, keeping a keen eye on all activity. This station was close to the border, and they knew it was a prime location for contraband like drugs, cigarettes, and pornography to cross over. This is what they were looking for. And Bibles. They lumped Bibles right in with the rest. Subversive material, they called it. Literature from the West that tried to brainwash their people.

The screech of the train brakes died away as the wheels on the train came to a halt. The locomotive engine puffed gently.

The engineer opened the sliding window beside him and, with a quick motion, threw a package out toward the waiting men. Ilie was on the package in a moment, and even though it was heavy, he quickly stuffed it into the sidecar. Then he and his driver took off. Ilie glanced back and saw another package come sailing out. The other man picked it up and left in the opposite direction. The engineer closed the sliding window and stepped to the door facing the station.

The cold air whipped past Ilie's face as they raced away from the station. More than once he turned to see if they were being followed, but he could see no one.

The single headlight stabbed into the darkness ahead of them. They had left the main road now, and the less traveled road was still covered in snow. The wind had picked up and the now-swirling snow in front of them reduced visibility. Ilie bent his head down and used the man's back in front of him as a shield.

They were traveling at a good speed, eager to get out of the cold and stash their cargo safely. Suddenly there was a bump as the sidecar hit something, and through the darkness, Ilie saw a black shape in the snow beside the road. The driver kept on going.

"You hit something!" Ilie tried to make himself heard. He bumped his head on the brother's back. "You hit something back there!"

His words were caught by the wind and flung away.

"Hey, I think you hit something back there on the road," Ilie said when they stopped inside the village.

"Hurry, get the package inside." The man had no time for conversation.

There was light inside the small building the villagers used for church services. Ilie had just picked up the package and started toward the building when the driver pulled away and disappeared into the night.

Soon the other motorcycle arrived. Someone came running out and took that package. Then the second motorcycle left as well.

Four men were gathered inside. They quickly cut open the heavy plastic that surrounded the packages and stacked the smaller packages against the front entry wall. Someone rolled up the heavy plastic and tied it with a string. The plastic was tossed onto the top shelf.

Abruptly the door was flung open. Policemen! The doorway was filled with faces.

Ilie's heart sank. They had been discovered! Immediately he began to pray.

"Where is the driver?" the head official asked coldly as the five officers filed into the entry.

"There is no driver here," one of the men replied.

"Passports!"

Everyone reached for their pockets.

"Get in there," the official ordered, indicating the main room. There was a shuffle of feet as they filed through the double doorway. Ilie was distinctly aware of the incriminating packages stacked alongside the wall, clearly in view of the officers.

One by one their passports were scrutinized. "Someone was hit on the road. Who was driving?"

They had hit someone? Was the person all right? Ilie's heart pounded heavily.

The other men shook their heads to indicate they knew nothing about it.

"You! Why are you here?" The official had sprung into investigative mode as soon as he saw Ilie's Romanian passport.

"I have come to visit," Ilie answered.

"When did you come?"

"I came yesterday." Yes, it had been yesterday when he had

arrived and arranged for the pickup of the Russian Bibles at the train station. He had been wearing the agreed–upon red and blue knitted cap so the engineer would recognize him. That was how it had been planned. This had not been the first such delivery.

Several of the officers were walking around the room, picking up songbooks and flipping through the pages.

"You are a spy." The words came harshly to Ilie. "You were sent by the Americans to infiltrate our country."

The verbal attack caught Ilie off guard, as it was meant to do. "No, no!" he said quickly. "I just came here to visit." But the officers were not persuaded so easily. Grabbing him by the arms, they hurried him out of the building. They did not even notice the packages stacked along the front entry wall. The Bibles were safe!

* * * * *

The cell was dark and chilly. Ilie stamped rhythmically on the floor to keep his circulation going. He tucked his hands under his armpits to try to warm his numbed fingers.

Approaching footsteps came down the corridor. They stopped in front of his cell door and the hatch slid open. The key turned in the lock and the door swung open.

What was it to be this time, Ilie wondered. Would someone else be put in for the night, pretending to be a prisoner, hoping to glean information that he didn't even know? Would it be another summons to that cold, impersonal room where an interrogator would pretend to be sympathetic with him, trying to get Ilie to say something against the Soviet government?

Or would it be one of the rough days? Hours of listening to rantings and ravings about how evil the Americans were and how you couldn't trust any foreigners?

It had been during one of those sessions that an officer had told him gleefully, "Your wife has denounced you. When she heard that you are in prison for killing a man on the road, she said she wants nothing more to do with you. You are a murderer!"

Even though Ilie knew it was not true, it still hurt. He had found out that the man they had hit had not died, but that did not matter to the officials.

"We took away all the Bibles, songbooks, and even the notebooks with handwritten copies of songs," the officer had mocked. "You Christians think you can carry on subversive activities and we will turn the other way! Absolutely not! There is no God, and our country will be better off once all you people are put away!"

During the four weeks of his incarceration, Ilie often wondered if he would be forgotten and simply rot in jail. That was what the officials wanted him to think. They told him nothing when he asked about a trial. Nothing.

It was hard to be jailed in a lonely, cold cell in another country, away from home. Ilie fought many battles against discouragement. He had read about people who were persecuted for being Christians, and Ilie knew the stories were true. He had always thrilled at the wonderful testimonies of God's people during their hard times.

But God didn't always seem so very close to him. The nights were long and cold. At times Ilie's prayers seemed to go no further than the ceiling of his cell. But gradually Ilie's persistent faith was rewarded, and he felt the presence of the Spirit with him. As he prayed and sang, he knew that, yes, God was there and loved him deeply.

So now, Ilie did not know what to expect from the guard who had come to summon him. His footsteps echoed in the corridor as he followed his escort into the examining room.

"Sign here." A paper was shoved toward him.

Ilie looked at the words. Dismissed? He was being released?

"Sign!"

Picking up the pen, Ilie signed the document.

.   .   .   .   .

"He took me to the train station," Ilie told Maria. "Made sure I was on the train and then left. No explanation. No apology."

"What I care about most is that you are safe at home," Maria's voice shook. "Sometimes I almost lost hope that I would ever see you again."

"Isn't it amazing that I was never caught with Bibles all those times I crossed the border? Thankfully, they found nothing incriminating while they investigated my history." Ilie tried to put the pieces of the puzzle together. "They must have verified my story that I had relatives in Cernauți and that I had not been the driver of the motorcycle that hit that man."

Chapter Thirteen

The Wolf Will Not Win

"There is no way." *Alexei,* the pastor visiting from the northern part of the Soviet Union, shook his head. "You cannot fight against the Soviet wolf and win."

"The wolf," *Slavic* repeated slowly. "The wolf is in a mighty battle against the Lion of Judah, but in my heart I know the wolf will not win." Slavic felt the words rise boldly inside him. His heart swelled. "Brother," he said, "our God is bigger than any wolf. We serve a Creator who can do mightier things than we even dream of."

"Show him." The voice of the Spirit that came to Slavic was quiet, yet insistent.

Show him? But they were to keep the very existence of the Bibles a top secret.

Again the voice spoke, "Show Alexei."

Slavic bit his lower lip and turned his head to look out the window. Warm sunshine streamed in through the window. The morning was turning toward noon.

"Would you like to see evidence that God has not forgotten us, and even though our government is becoming harsher, we are not standing alone? Do you want to see something that is evidence that there must be hundreds, if not thousands, of Christians praying for us?"

Alexei turned his head toward Slavic. "What do you mean, see something? Sure, my faith needs some kind of confirmation, though I can't think what you could show me that is relevant."

"If you are willing to be blindfolded, go somewhere in my car, have the blindfold taken off to feast your eyes on proof that we are not forgotten, and then be brought back here blindfolded, I will show you something. Something that will help you realize God has not forgotten us." As Slavic spoke, he felt an inner surge of faith course through him.

"Sounds dramatic," Alexei said with a wry grin.

Slavic shrugged. "It is dramatic. And it's proof."

"Okay. Let's go."

The small car turned onto side roads as they zigzagged through the streets of Cernauți. Slavic intentionally made several turns to keep his passenger confused.

Alexei said little, his hat pulled low over his face and his eyes blinded by the scarf Slavic had given him when they were seated in the car.

The row of outdoor storage sheds guarded by a pair of iron gates was hardly unusual. Such sheds were common in any Soviet city, and the people renting the sheds used them as repair shops or simply to store goods. The guard in the small booth nodded as Slavic drove up. He was registered to use Unit 57.

"Okay, take your blindfold off," Slavic instructed as he stopped the motor. "I will get out, and when I have unlocked the door, come in."

The heavy metal door squealed slightly as Slavic opened

one side. He would have to get some oil and lubricate that hinge. Alexei joined him inside. A single electric bulb hung from the ceiling and dimly illuminated the shed. The usual boxes and storage items were stashed along the wall. A workbench with several tools was in the back underneath the barred window. Slavic closed the door and locked it from the inside. Then motioning to his companion, he went toward the narrow set of stairs against one wall.

The storage sheds were built on the side of a hill, so it had been easy to build the basement under the main floor. The basement had a small window looking out over the steep ravine behind the shed, and at first Alexei could not understand what he was looking at. Why were crates stacked up on top of cement blocks to keep them off the damp floor? What was in them?

Slavic pulled a wooden crate toward him. He opened the top and the two men looked inside. Through the clear plastic Alexei saw the black books. In gold letters, the word *Biblia* leaped up at him. Rows of Bibles! He looked in surprise at Slavic. Then he looked at the other boxes.

Slavic nodded his head. "All of them." He opened another box. New Testaments.

Silently Alexei counted. Twenty-three boxes. He counted the Bibles inside the open box. Two rows of ten made twenty. Twenty times twenty-three. Four hundred sixty Bibles! And the boxes that held New Testaments held even more. The numbers were staggering.

"But who? How? Where did they all come from?"

Slavic smiled and shook his head. "You do not want to know how they came here. I don't want to know. You know information like that is dangerous. What I do know is that people in the West have heard about the rigid restrictions our government has put on us. They have been moved by God to send these Bibles to us."

Alexei reached out and laid his hand on top of the plastic where the Bibles lay stacked underneath. His lips moved silently, and he kept shaking his head. Taking a deep sigh, he turned back to his friend. "You are right. God has not forgotten us. The wolf is not winning."

.   .   .   .   .   .

Slavic waited until the passengers boarded his bus. Then he closed the door and, checking his mirror, pulled the bus out into the traffic. Slavic enjoyed his work as a bus driver. He met interesting people and got to know the streets of his route quite well. This morning the bus was not crowded. Most of the workers were already at their jobs, and the people on the bus were mostly pensioners who had wisely waited until the crowds diminished before going to see their children or setting about their business.

Brown leaves blew against the curbs. Winter would soon be here once more.

At the next stop several people got off, and two men in business suits boarded. They paid their fare and seated themselves in the seat right behind Slavic. They were obviously government officials. It was not hard for Slavic to place the two men. Not only were they dressed quite well, but their mannerisms also suggested they were accustomed to being in control. Their eyes had a steely glint about them.

There was nothing terribly unusual about their presence.

People of all sorts used the bus, although the high ranking officials were usually chauffeured about in black Volgas.

The two men did not get off at the next bus stop. Nor at the next. In fact, they stayed on the bus until Slavic had deposited his last passengers.

It was the end of his shift, although it was only midday. He would be glad to get back home and catch some sleep before his next shift began at midnight.

He sensed that something might keep him from his usual schedule. The two men met his gaze in the rearview mirror, and just as Slavic drove his bus into the company's parking lot, one of them spoke.

"We are taking you in for questioning." The words were terse and clipped. He flipped his lapel open and Slavic saw his badge.

He said nothing, but parked the bus in the usual place. He turned to face the men.

"We have been trailing you. We know what you are doing." Again the words were clipped short.

During his ride in the back seat of the Volga, Slavic felt his heart racing. His prayers were silent cries for help and strength to face what lay ahead.

. . . . .

"Where do you get your information that another shipment is coming?"

"Someone informs me," Slavic replied evasively.

"What is his name?"

"It is not a he."

"Don't play games with us!" shouted the officer as he struck the desk with his fist. "What is her name?"

"*Natasha.*"

"What is her last name?"

"I don't know. I don't know where she lives. I don't know where she comes from. I just know we call her Natasha. That may not even be her real name," Slavic told his questioner.

"We have ways of making you talk," the officer spat venomously. "You must know how you are getting the Bibles. You must know how they are being brought across the border! Don't you understand? These books are illegal. You are breaking the law! You are guilty of conspiring with the Americans as a spy. That is treason!"

Yes, Slavic had heard that before. In fact, he had been hearing it daily for seven days.

Was it only a week ago that he had been brought in here, directly from his bus route? Only a week, but it seemed as though the days and nights stretched out in timeless spaces that had no hands on the clock.

Did his children know where he was? *Yulia* was capable of taking care of the needs of her brother John, and since they were both students in the university, their days probably went on as before. But at night when they came home to the apartment, did they suspect that their father was incarcerated?

For the first time since his wife died eight years before, Slavic felt relief that she was no longer on the earth. He knew it would have been extremely difficult for her to cope with his absence without word as to his whereabouts.

Slavic thought of other brethren who had disappeared, some to face a rigged court and others to disappear into the great unknown. What would his fate be?

The interrogation didn't vary much from day to day. Who were the people involved? How did they get the Bibles?

At first Slavic was not sure just how much the officers knew. But as they continued to question him, he gleaned that they knew very little except that occasionally Bibles were delivered to him.

Incidentally, that was all he knew! Occasionally someone named Natasha would come to him after church and say, "More food is coming." Then she would disappear. Now he was doubly glad he had never tried to find out her identity.

All he knew was that an erratic stream of Bibles came flowing out of somewhere. Oh, yes, he had often pondered about the whereabouts and prayed often for the courageous people who had handled them along the way. He also continually thanked God for the people who had started the precious books on their path to the believers in the Soviet Union. Like Alexei, there were many whose faith had been strengthened to learn of the caring and sharing hearts of those who were providing Bibles.

Some days the questions rained on him with sharp, angry words. Other days the questions came in wily, pacifying tones meant to ease his guard and have him divulge information. But no matter how the questions came, he could only give the same answers over and over, "I don't know."

Alone in his cell, his thoughts often traveled back to Alexei's words. "You cannot fight against the wolf and win." He remembered his own valiant words of rebuttal and the joy he had in showing the stash of Bibles to his skeptical friend. He remembered how they had prayed together and how Alexei had thanked him for allowing him to see the Bibles. He had said he would go back to working with his fellowship, strengthened and encouraged that the "wolf" was not winning. But sometimes in the dark and lonely nights, Slavic was not too sure the wolf was not winning. His thoughts wanted to run amok and rest among the dark figures of discouragement and, yes, even despair. His prison cell seemed far more real than his nebulous faith.

"I will believe in you, Lord!" Slavic spoke out in anguish more than once. "In my weakness, help me!"

Through his troubled thoughts, words from his own sermons came back to him, words of encouragement he had given his congregation as he had told them about the prophets of old and the plight of the early Christians. "They trusted in God when they had no earthly reason to trust!" He could still almost hear himself say those very words. He had believed them then.

"I still believe," he cried out in anguish. "Lord Jesus, help my unbelief."

Then, more than once in the dark and cold of the night, through the uncertainty of his future, through all the doubts that wanted to win the battles in his mind, Slavic knew that God did really care and had not forsaken him. He began to actually look forward to the times in his cell when he was touched by the presence of God and could feel the overwhelming power and love that comes from knowing he was not forgotten by God. At those times the wolf turned tail and fled as the presence of the Lion drove out all fear.

Slavic was sentenced to three years hard labor for being involved with "propaganda" from enemy countries. The three years of poor food, hard work, and filthy conditions were not easy. Still, after he was released, he became involved in printing songbooks inside the Soviet Union and poured himself once more into God's work. He knew that the Lion was stronger than any wolf.

Chapter Fourteen

Gaining Trust

Once more *Zaharia* opened the small piece of paper with the handwritten address. There was no name, for he had memorized that. He was looking for house number 212 on Gluschova Street. He peered intently at the ordinary-looking house in front of him.

A light shone from the front entry, and he thought there might be another light shining out into the side yard. He reached out and knocked on the outside of the yard gate.

There was an immediate outcry from a watch dog, and Zaharia winced as he heard the deep-throated barking from a huge dog inside the fence. There was certainly no need for further knocking. The dog was all the alarm anyone inside the house might need.

A shadow crossed in front of the light in the enclosed porch. Someone parted the lace curtain and peered out into the evening.

Zaharia shifted his feet. The dog continued to bark and lunged against the chest-high wooden fence.

The door opened a crack and a voice called to the dog. The dog subsided into silence.

"Yes?" a man's voice questioned.

"Hello! I am looking for Pavel," Zaharia spoke loudly enough for the man to hear distinctly.

"My name is *Pasha*."

Zaharia waited. He knew that Pasha was the informal name for Pavel, and he was willing to wait to see if this was indeed the place he had been seeking.

When there was no remark from him, the man asked, "Where do you live?"

"I come from the south."

Pavel stepped out of his house and closed the door behind him. The light from the entry framed his silhouette, but it was impossible for Zaharia to see his face.

Pavel walked to the board fence and opened the gate a crack. He studied the newcomer's face as well as he could in the darkness. He scanned the street behind the young man.

"What is your name?"

"My name is Zaharia." He was glad now for the Bible name that his parents had chosen for their third son twenty-one years ago.

"Why do you come here?"

"I was told that possibly there is some food here."

Pavel did not immediately answer. Then he said slowly, "Food?" his voice rising in inflection.

Zaharia nodded and continued to wait.

"You come from the south, yes?"

"Yes."

"And you come to my house for food?"

Once more Zaharia nodded.

The headlights of a car from the intersection came toward them.

"Step inside," Pavel directed. As soon as Zaharia was inside, he closed the gate. The car drove on past.

"How did you come?" Pavel continued.

"I traveled by train."

"From what city?"

"From just outside Chişinău."

"How long did it take you to travel?" This question came quickly.

Zaharia did not hesitate. "Five days."

The answer seemed to satisfy Pavel. He nodded slightly.

"And you came for food?"

"Yes. I heard that there might be some spiritual food available here. At this house," he added hopefully.

"Come inside," Pavel invited. "I will get you something to eat. You must be hungry after all that travel."

The inside of Pavel's house was very similar to Zaharia's own home. He met Pavel's wife *Ana* and smiled at their three little children who were waiting around the kitchen table with their mother.

"Thank you," Zaharia nodded gratefully as Pavel added another chair to the table.

"Let us pray," Pavel said, and the children and their mother all stood respectfully. "Zaharia, will you pray?"

Looking around at the standing family, he answered, "Yes, if you would like me to."

Pavel nodded.

Zaharia bowed his head. "Lord God, I thank you for safety on my journey and for bringing me to this family. I thank you for Jesus and for the salvation that only comes in the name of your Son. I also thank you for providing the food that is here on this table. I thank you for the people who have worked to prepare the food. May your blessing be on this house and on the people who live here and work for you. I pray this in the name of the Father and the Son and the Holy Spirit. Amen."

The children joined in saying "amen" and they all sat down.

The meal was simple. A big dish of fried potatoes was placed in the center of the table, and a cucumber salad was served on the side. A slice of black bread lay on each plate. Although nothing elaborate, it was well-made and tasty. Zaharia ate hungrily. After five days of eating sandwiches and some dry cheese, it was good to share hot food with this family.

"What is your work?" Pavel asked.

"I just graduated from the university and work as a mechanical engineer for the collective farm."

Pavel speared another piece of potato and looked intently at the young man. "That is my job as well. May I ask you a few questions about your work?"

The questions directed at him reminded Zaharia of the oral test he had taken in order to get his degree. Pavel fired off technical questions about motors, including a few Zaharia could not answer. Nothing more was asked about why he was there. No mention was made of his earlier statement that he had come to this house in order to get food.

"We have no spare room, but you are welcome to sleep here on the sofa," Pavel invited.

"Thank you," Zaharia said gratefully, stifling a yawn. "You are very kind."

That night he went to sleep immediately. He felt so grateful to be able to stretch out and relax in a prone position. The train had not been a very satisfactory place to sleep.

. . . . .

"Tell me about your church," Pavel requested one evening as they left the collective farm and headed back to Pavel's house. "Who are your leaders?"

Zaharia told him. He explained that the church numbered around a hundred members and that it had been established for several decades.

Each day Zaharia went with Pavel to work and helped him in the mechanic shop. He knew he was being tested, and he asked very few questions. He did what he could and waited.

He went with Pavel to the midweek prayer meeting. He prayed with the believers there. Several of the men spoke to him, and he felt comfortable with the group. He guessed he was being scrutinized and tested before he was going to be fully trusted.

A break came when he saw a Christian newsletter in Pavel's house. It was secretly printed and circulated among the believers, and Zaharia was able to point out a picture of a group of young people from his church along with an article written by one of his pastors.

Pavel looked long and hard at the picture, glancing at Zaharia as though convincing himself that the young man in the picture was the same boy standing in his living room.

. . . . .

"Tonight we go by car to see a friend," Pavel told Zaharia one evening after supper.

As the headlights beamed two streams of light into the

night, Pavel said simply, "I know a brother who sometimes gets Bibles."

Zaharia did not respond. He did not know if he should ask questions or not, but he felt a surge of excitement. Was he closer to his goal? Was Pavel beginning to trust him?

"Sometimes," Pavel repeated, "we can find Bibles."

"I am happy for you," Zaharia said simply.

"The spiritual food that we need is being supplied by the grace of God. It is through much difficulty that we have been able to get any at all. Many people suffer for this privilege."

Zaharia nodded.

"Please wait," Pavel said after they stopped in front of a village house.

He was gone for about half an hour before the door opened and Pavel waved him in. An elderly couple lived in the house. The man's hair were white and full and the woman's eyes had the look of patient suffering in them.

"Why did you come?" The old man's voice was cool, yet not totally unfriendly.

"I have heard that sometimes there are Bibles here, and we have a great need for Bibles in our town," Zaharia said honestly.

"How did you find out about Bibles being here?"

"A brother who was visiting relatives told my father that occasionally Bibles were coming in from the West. He gave me Pavel's address, so I came."

His answers were the same ones he had given Pavel, but he felt once more that he was being tested. Would they trust him? Was there still some suspicion as to whether he was an informer? Zaharia was not sure, but he kept committing his trip into God's hands. He knew what he had come for, and he was not willing to go home without Bibles if there were some to be had.

The old man closed his eyes for a few moments, and then rising slowly, he said to Pavel, "Come." Turning to Zaharia, he said, "Wait here, please."

While they were gone, the lady engaged him in friendly conversation, asking about his family and church.

Eventually Pavel came back into the room carrying a wooden crate in his arms. He set the crate on the floor in front of the sofa. The old man took his seat and pulled back the packing straw. Underneath the straw Zaharia saw them—two stacks of Bibles. Taking one in his hands, the old man handed it to Zaharia. "Is this what you came for?"

Zaharia could not speak. He simply nodded and carefully began turning pages.

"Take them," the old man invited generously. "Take them to your fellowship, young man. This is the Word of God. I know you will treat it as the treasure it is."

His voice choked with emotion as he continued, "These books have come here only through much difficulty for many people. Even I have already seen the inside of a prison cell for two years because of being involved in the work. Please be extra careful and never tell anyone where you have gotten them."

"By the grace of God, I will never tell," Zaharia said humbly. "I thank you on behalf of my fellowship back home for this tremendous gift. I will guard them well."

"Are you aware of what could happen if you are caught transporting these Bibles? They are not printed inside the Soviet Union, and the authorities will know that. They are known to go to great lengths to make people talk." It was evident to Zaharia that the old man spoke from experience. The lines on his face showed signs of deep suffering. "It could be compared to carrying materials to produce nuclear weapons. The officials count it much the same."

Zaharia nodded. The gravity of the situation was not escaping him.

. . . . . .

"Where did you get your Bible?" The woman's voice was sharp with surprise as she looked at her friend's new possession.

Zaharia strained to hear without making it too obvious that he was interested.

They were standing in the front yard of the home where they had conducted the Sunday morning service. Daffodils nodded alongside the house, and even though the sun wasn't shining, it was definitely getting warmer.

"Well," the first speaker said cautiously, "someone said there were Bibles under the bench in the front entry. I could hardly believe it, but I went to look, and sure enough, there were several there. I saw some other people with Bibles, so I took this one. I asked Brother Vanya and he said it was okay."

"Do you think there are any left?" The second woman started toward the door of the house.

"Oh, no! They are all gone. The last ones were taken even as I was standing there."

The woman's shoulders sagged in disappointment.

"I will lend you this one," the first lady said generously. "As close as we live, we can share this one."

"Yes!"

Zaharia looked intently at the second woman. He would try to make sure she got a Bible after he returned from his next trip.

"It is all right," he had assured his mother after his return trip. "God has protected me and I believe He will continue to do so." When he showed the twenty Bibles he had brought on the train, his parents had been greatly moved and immediately began to praise the Lord.

The first trip was followed by another one several months later. That time Zaharia had been able to bring back only four, but on the following trip he had been given as many as he could carry. Two bags with twenty Bibles each were heavy, yet the strong young man had been glad to carry the precious books back to his community.

Then he had gone again, and that time Zaharia had taken the ten-day trip in vain. There had been no Bibles.

"We don't know why," Pavel told him. By this time the two had become close friends. "We don't know if someone got caught or what happened, but as you well know, very little information is passed on to anyone. We did hear of a brother in another church who was taken away and not heard of again. Only God knows if that has anything to do with the absence of Bibles."

Several months later he had tried again. God rewarded his diligence, and he was loaded with Bibles on that trip.

.   .   .   .   .

"A young man like you should get married," one of the church women half-teased him one day. "You are good-looking and hardworking enough for any girl."

Zaharia grinned good-naturedly, but he was not making any plans for marriage. He was quite content to stay at home with his parents and go to work on the collective farm.

However, the real reason was that he knew it was better and easier for him to take the trips as a single man. He knew that leaving a wife behind would make it more difficult for both of them, and he also knew that if he should get caught with contraband, he would not have to worry about having forsaken a wife. No, marriage could wait.

Taking an average of six trips a year, Zaharia continued his work for four years. Most of the trips were fruitful, but occasionally there was nothing there for him to bring home. In time, hundreds of Bibles found their way into the eager hands of the believers.

.   .   .   .   .

One evening Zaharia came home after work and saw his brother *Gheorghe's* car in the yard.

"Hey, brother!" Zaharia greeted his oldest brother affectionately.

Gheorghe had not lived at home for more than five years. Much to his parents' dismay and grief, he had drifted away from the church and had begun training as a police officer. Married to a non-Christian, it looked outwardly as though he was prospering. He already owned a car and had been allotted a nice apartment.

"Zaharia!" Gheorghe grinned broadly. He slapped his younger brother affectionately on the shoulder.

It was late that evening when Gheorghe followed Zaharia

outside into the summer evening.

"What are you up to? Are you having a problem?" The question came bluntly from Gheorghe.

Zaharia was immediately on guard. "Why do you ask? I am working at the garage on the collective farm."

With the keen look of a trained policeman, Gheorghe said, "I don't mean that."

Zaharia said nothing.

Then Gheorghe's eyes softened as he looked at his younger brother. "Listen, if there is something going on, stop doing it. I don't know what it is or anything, but something is going on."

"What do you mean? I mean, how do you know?" Zaharia felt more comfortable asking now that Gheorghe had dropped his officer look and was talking like a brother.

"Several times different officers in the force have asked me about my family. Just yesterday one asked me if I had a brother named Zaharia. I know the questions are meant to alert me that someone is suspicious of someone in my family. When they asked about having a brother named Zaharia, I knew it was you."

"Don't tell me. I don't want to know, but if you are doing something, I am warning you. You are being watched."

Zaharia was silent.

"Take this seriously. I have worked with these people for two years now and know the procedures. They warned me only because you are my brother. If I had no friends in the police force, there would be no warning."

Long into the night, Zaharia prayed and asked God what he should do.

Zaharia did not stop. He continued to make his trips north and brought Bibles back whenever he could.

"How could I stop when there were so many needs in our area for more Bibles?" Zaharia told me. "I tried being more careful, sometimes buying tickets on the way to destinations and buying the next ticket at that station. I tried to find out if I was being followed, and as far as I know, no one was trailing me.

"For two more years, I continued to travel before our source mysteriously dried up. During the 1980s we had greater freedom and I helped to print Bibles right here in Moldova. We printed and distributed over 10,000 Bibles."

Zaharia did get married when he was in his thirties. Now, after the revolution, he is a part of a large and active church where he stills marvels at how easily anyone can get Bibles.

Chapter Fifteen

Special Truck Deliveries

The dump truck lumbering down the dirt road bounced over the frozen ruts. The driver kept peering through the windshield, staring intently at the houses. "19 Railroad Street," Pavel kept murmuring to himself. "Number 19."

He had no address written on paper. He had memorized it. Yes, he was on Railroad Street and number 19 should be close at hand.

There it was, house number 19. He slowed his truck down. Then he noticed an A after the 19. He stopped and looked quizzically at the next house. Number 19.

There were two 19s. One 19 and one 19A.

His contact had not told him that. He had just told him, "Take the goods to Railroad Street, house number 19." No description, no further instructions.

Pavel was tired. Driving a dump truck all the way back from north of Moscow to the southern part of the Soviet Union would be stressful under normal circumstances, but this load to deliver on the way home made it even more stressful.

He had started his journey southward three days ago. Driving ten hours a day, he had made good time, but he was eager to unload and continue home, another long day's drive.

He rubbed his chin and stared at the houses. How could he tell which was the right one? There was no way to guess, and his weary mind wanted to tell him that the first house would be the obvious one, but something else told him that, no, the one simply marked "19" was the correct one.

Well, he would find out. He kept the motor idling and knocked on the front gate of 19A. There was no answer to his repeated knocking, so he opened the gate.

He stepped up to the front door and knocked again. He heard a small dog begin to bark inside, and a white curtain moved inside the entrance door.

"Hello!" Pavel called out, knocking again.

Inside, the dog was quiet. There was no movement of the curtain.

He tried the latch. It was not locked, so he opened the door a crack and called again, "Hello!"

The curtain moved again. The door opened slightly and a middle-aged woman looked at him. "What do you want?" she asked sharply.

Pavel smiled. "I have some goods to deliver to you. Sent from the north." There, that should do it. The woman should realize the code words he was using. Perhaps now she would be friendly and help him get rid of the goods.

"I don't know anything about it." The woman's voice was sharp, and she began closing the door.

"Wait!" Pavel said. "Yes, you do know! I mean, there is something that the brothers, I mean, the people north of here said you will understand when I come!" He realized with dismay that he was not sounding very convincing.

"Go away! I don't know you!"

Despair wanted to clutch at Pavel's heart. He was stuck! There was no alternate plan.

"Who lives in house 19? Maybe they were expecting goods." Pavel's voice was hoarse in his desperation.

"Why are you here?" The woman's voice was getting higher pitched. "Are you drunk? Get away from here."

She stared at him with disgust.

When Pavel saw her look at his clothes and dirty hands, he realized that he must be quite a sight. Taking a slow, deep breath, he began again.

"Madam, I'm sorry. I realize I must look quite rough, but I have been traveling for three days in my truck. I haven't had time to shave and wash, and just this afternoon I had to change a tire on my truck. I realize I don't look very reputable, but I really do have a load, uh … goods, to deliver to this address.

"A brother told me to bring it here. He said there are believers living here who would take the load."

The sharp eyes bored into Pavel's tired face. Then with a decisive shake, the woman said, "I know nothing about it."

She thinks I am a secret agent, Pavel realized with dismay, *someone who has come here to spy on the activities of this house.* As the door began to close again, Pavel said boldly, "If you don't accept the goods, I will dump them on the street in front of your house and leave. Then you will be asked questions!"

"Are you a believer?" The question came in a softer tone.

"Yes," Pavel said quickly. Was he really getting through to her?

"Thank you, God, for bringing me here," he began praying

aloud. "Please move this lady's heart to take what has been sent to her. If there are others who need what I bring, open up the doors for them to receive it as well. You know the sincerity of my heart, Lord, and I give you all the praise. In the name of Jesus Christ, the Son of God, Amen."

"Amen," the woman's voice echoed softly. "I will open the gate and you can drive around the back."

. . . . .

"God, you never told me I would have to try to convince anyone to take the Bibles," Pavel said out loud as he steered the truck through the night. "When I agreed to bring the Bibles, I pictured all these people with ready, open arms, glad to receive your Word that has been brought into the country through so much difficulty." Praying out loud was a good way to keep his weary mind awake. "Thank you for convincing that woman I was genuine and not some spy. It was rewarding to see her eyes when she saw the huge stack of Bibles unloaded into her shed."

By the time he had driven the truck inside the yard and uncovered the pallet of Bibles all wrapped in black plastic, help had arrived in the form of two young boys.

Slashing open the plastic with his knife, Pavel had opened a package and showed it to the woman. She gasped. Raising her hands toward heaven, she clasped them together in grateful worship.

The boys had stowed the packages inside a shed just in time, for Pavel saw his tires beginning to sink into the frozen ground.

"The septic tank!" The woman's cry of distress had horrified Pavel. He had sprinted to the cab and gotten out of there just in time.

There had been no time for civilities, no time to sit and have a cup of tea or something to eat with the lady and her household. Speed was of utmost importance, and if some of the neighbors would become inquisitive enough to drop by, it was much better that he should be gone already.

"Thank you, Lord!" Pavel prayed. "Thank you. Maybe I can find a place along the highway to pull off and sleep now that I only have the designated load for the factory back in *Chişinău*."

The tired trucker pulled to the side of the road and went to sleep. Another one of many loads of Bibles had been delivered. One more link in the chain to get God's Word into the hands of the hungry people.

.　.　.　.　.

Red October Street. House number 3. Yes, here it was, the address given for the delivery.

Although Pavel had made numerous Bible deliveries, it was still always a relief for him to actually find the address and know that he would soon be able to unload the goods he was carrying.

Once more he marveled at how the doors continually opened for him to be involved in the Bible work. His constant trips across the Soviet Union gave multiple opportunities for the network to use his and other Christian truck drivers' services. It was somewhat ironic and yet in keeping with God's principles that the very people willing to take risks in transporting Bibles were the most qualified to be driving transport trucks.

"You people are the only ones we can depend on," his foreman had once told Pavel. "You guys are the only ones who are reliable. The rest are a bunch of drunks."

It was true. In Pavel's native Moldova, the majority of the men were so addicted to alcohol that they did not qualify to be truck drivers. Pavel chuckled to himself. If "you people" meant the Christians, that was fine. It did not matter what term was used to describe the believers if it left a good testimony. You people. That was good. Praise God for the "you people."

It was the perfect setup. The Christian truck drivers were sent out all over the Soviet Union to deliver and pick up loads. Their travels were the perfect way to connect the dots for Bible deliveries. Pavel was not sure how many of his fellow truckers were involved in the work. They did not discuss it among themselves. Secrecy was paramount in case the network was discovered.

But it worked for him. He was given addresses, he memorized them, and he delivered the loads. There were many times he could have honestly told any inspectors that he did not even know what was on his truck. Not only were the literature pallets that often contained Bibles and other printed material wrapped and sealed, but even the goods the state gave him to transport were sealed inside containers. The lowly truckers were not privy to information about the contents.

This time, Pavel knew he was transporting dinnerware. Lots of it was being sent to his native city of Chişinău. This trip had taken him right past a way station for the Bible network people, so he had stopped. A man with a forklift had loaded a pallet of something, presumably Bibles, on top of his load, told him the address, and waved him on.

Now here he was, knocking on the front door.

There was no answer, so he knocked again. The strangled cries of a watch dog straining against his chain came from behind the house. From the deep sound of the bark, Pavel concluded it was a very big dog, and he hoped the chain would hold.

Repeated knockings brought no answer. Obviously, this would not be an easy delivery.

Pavel loved when everything moved like clockwork: he arrived, the people were expecting him, he was unloaded and on his way again in minutes, the precious cargo safely delivered. Of course, there were these times when no one was at home or when he had to somehow convince the people that he really did have something for them and could be trusted.

"Lord, show me what to do," he prayed now. One thing he had learned, or was learning, was to be continually in prayer. There was no way he could find his own way out of these predicaments. He had learned that God was much more dependable than his own intuitions.

The silent house seemed to mock him. The curtained windows stared at him blankly, and the brooding house sat silently in the yard. "Please, God," he prayed and tried the door knob. It did not turn.

"Try the back," God seemed to whisper.

Cautiously edging around the corner, Pavel saw the dog.

Now seeing the intruder, the dog lunged toward the truck driver, his barks coming out in savage wheezes as the chain tightened his leather collar.

No use trying to sweet talk this one into friendliness, Pavel decided. He tried to ignore the vicious sounds and went toward the back door. To his relief, it was not locked. He stepped inside the enclosed back porch and called out, "Hello!" There was no answer. He tried the door into what was obviously the kitchen. It, too, yielded to his entrance.

Pavel kept calling out, hoping there would be some answering voice. He turned the corner. There on the sofa lay a blanket-covered form. Someone was at home! Relief flooded through him.

"Hello!" he called again, moving across the floor toward the sofa.

The blanket moved.

"Get out!" The old man's voice still had a vestige of authority in the quavering words, and the wide eyes under the gray mop of hair were still sharp.

"Wait! Please! I can explain!" Pavel knew he needed to speak quickly. "I am sent here with something for this household. A gift."

"Get out!" The words were even stronger this time. "I don't know you."

"I am sent here by the brothers. I have something for you." Pavel did not retreat.

"Who are you?"

"Pavel."

The eyes bored suspiciously into him. It was obvious that the old man was not going to be convinced easily. Spreading his hands outward, Pavel began to pray. He asked God to bless the house and all who lived here. He asked God to continue to open the way for His children to learn more about

Him and to bless the people of this village with the Gospel.

"Who are you?"

A woman's voice from the kitchen startled him. He turned to face a puzzled lady staring at him from the kitchen doorway. She looked at the old man on the sofa and crossed the room to his side. She smoothed his wild hair.

"I can explain. I am Pavel and I have something to deliver to this house. I knocked and knocked and there was no answer, so I tried the back door and came in." Motioning with his hand toward the old man, Pavel continued, "He does not seem to understand what I have or who I am."

"Tata is very old and sometimes it takes him some time to figure out what's going on." She smiled at Pavel. "I know who you are. We just had no idea when you would arrive."

"It's okay," she said soothingly to her father. "He is a brother."

"I know," he replied. "I could tell by his prayer." He turned toward Pavel. "I need about thirty minutes to get the boys here to unload. Can you wait that long?"

Pavel nodded. "I will drive around the block. When I return, could you have the gate open? I don't have much, but it will be good to have lots of help to do the unloading quickly."

"May God bless you richly for your work," the woman said gratefully to Pavel. "I pray for all of you workers daily."

"It is a privilege I have to work for my Lord," Pavel said simply. "And may He bless you for the work you do to get the Bibles into the hands of the people."

She nodded, smiled, and clasped her hands together, lifting them up slightly.

Chapter Sixteen

Into Their Hands

Miriam placed the pen on the table and spread her fingers on the table top. She flexed each finger separately, trying to ignore the twinges of arthritis that had begun to plague her of late. Looking out the window into the backyard, she watched the golden fingers of the sun steal through the branches of the fruit trees. The apple trees were just now coming into full bloom and the cherry trees had already lost their pinkish petals. "Lord, bless your trees with a good harvest," she prayed.

Her mind flew to the underground storage space in the backyard where the potatoes and other vegetables were kept during winter. At the moment it held nothing but potatoes; the pumpkins, squash, and beets were gone.

"But thank you for the potatoes," Miriam said under her breath. She pushed away the worrisome thoughts that wanted to crowd in on her this glorious spring morning, thoughts of poverty and want and of trying to carefully ration out the meager food supply for herself and her husband.

Returning once more to the task at hand, she picked up her pen and, paying close attention to the words, began copying from the handwritten notebook in front of her. The Gospel of

John she had borrowed showed signs of heavy use. The pages of the notebook bore thumb marks at the edges, and the cover was worn as well. But it was a part of the Bible! Miriam thrilled at the thought that she was able to borrow the book long enough to copy it into her own notebook.

Times in the Soviet Union were hard. The collectivization had already pushed the farmers and common folk to the edge of desperation. With the government taking more than half of the harvest each year, very little was left for the winter. Even though they were in their fifties, Miriam and *Alexandru* were not spared from being forced to give from their garden, and without the occasional wheat and barley that Alexandru was allowed to bring back from the collective farm, Miriam was not sure how they would have survived the winter.

But now she had a copy of the Gospel of John! Pushing away all distractions, she began copying the third chapter. As her pen scratched across the paper, she once more thrilled at the account of Nicodemus coming to visit Jesus at night. The words seemed to have a life of their own as she wrote the familiar yet wonderful verses.

Perhaps when she was finished with this Gospel, she could borrow the book of Acts from someone and copy it. She would love to have the story of the experiences of the first church. How she always thrilled to hear about the work of the Holy Spirit among the believers. More than once she had longed to read for herself just how it was recorded. There was a copy somewhere among the members of the church, Miriam knew, perhaps even more than one copy.

In their church of over two hundred people, Miriam knew of only three complete Bibles. Two of the pastors each had one, and she had heard that someone else had one too. The rest had portions of handwritten copies, laboriously written and passed around and recopied by many.

Finding time to copy was difficult enough. Not many of the villagers had extra time on hand. Their jobs, their families, and their gardens took most of their waking hours.

But today was Sunday afternoon, and that was when Miriam tried to make time to do her copying. Time was of the essence, however, for there was such a demand from others who were impatiently waiting for their turn at copying.

In the background Miriam heard the sound of a motorcycle approaching. The main street of the village ran right in front of their house, and it was not uncommon for a motorcycle to be using the road. She did pause for a moment, though, as she heard the motor slow to an idle and stop in front of their house.

She saw Alexandru leave the bench outside in the sunlight where he had been resting and disappear around the corner of the house. She heard voices and was preparing to get up to greet whoever had come to see them when she saw her husband and another man round the corner of the house again.

It was Pavel. Pavel *Corni*, the pastor from the city of *Minsk*. Miriam watched as the two men settled themselves on the bench. Well, what had brought him out here? Miriam was curious, but the task at hand beckoned to her, and she went back to her copying.

Pavel and Alexandru had been childhood friends. Miriam had often heard her husband speak about his younger years, and Pavel was mentioned more than once. When Pavel had been chosen as a pastor, he had become quite busy, and the old friends rarely saw each other now. The couple had often prayed for Pavel because they knew it was not easy to be a minister during the communist era. The state was doing its best to stop the growth of the church.

Miriam wished she had some tea to brew for their guest. That was the hospitable thing to do. But they had no more tea. Even though they had been sipping weak tea all winter, they had finally used up the last of it.

She heard the men talking.

"No," Alexandru was saying, "we were not able to produce the daily quota of milk, so we are being fined."

Miriam knew about that. The collective farm manager had been severely criticized and fined when the milk production had dropped below acceptable levels. Never mind that the feed and hay had been severely depleted when a large amount had been taken to supply another dairy. Never mind that the cows were so skinny and hungry that their incessant bawling nearly drove the workers to distraction. Somewhere, some-one had decided that they should have been producing more milk, and when it didn't happen, someone had to take the blame. That someone had been the manager.

"He'll probably lose his job," Alexandru said with a resigned shake of his head.

Then there was silence.

Miriam began copying verse sixteen. "For God so loved the world, that he gave his only begotten Son, that whosoever believeth in him should not perish, but have everlasting life."

"Thank you, Lord!" Miriam's heart began to sing as she penned those wonderful words. She felt tears gather in the corners of her eyes. What a wonderful gift God had given to her and the whole world!

The conversation outside faded in the background as she continued to copy. She heard the murmur of the men's voices and was only dimly aware of what they were talking about. The economic times, the weather, and the trials of life were all common topics. But here in these blessed words was life!

Miriam remembered when these words had first meant something to her. When she had attended the wedding of a classmate as a young girl, the speaker had clearly spoken about Jesus, the Messiah and Saviour of the world. That had planted the seed, and Miriam had found herself repeatedly drawn to meetings in a house where the small group of believers met as often as they could to pray and worship.

There was an earnestness and urgency in the preaching. Time was short and life uncertain. For Miriam, that was all too evident. Funerals were common in their village, and the reality of life was many times accentuated by the starkness of death.

So Miriam had repented. Kneeling on the floor of the house where the meetings were being held, she had sobbed for her sins and accepted the healing and saving love of Jesus Christ.

God had brought a serious-minded man into her life, and when she and Alexandru had gotten married, Miriam felt so blessed. The four children born to them were all grown now and had homes of their own, but the blessedness of her life in Christ continued to inspire her.

She saw Pavel stand and realized that he was probably getting ready to leave. She should at least offer him a drink of water. But the words of John kept drawing her on and on in her work.

Suddenly she heard Alexandru call her name. "Miriam!"

Looking out her window, she saw the two men facing each other.

"Yes?" she answered loudly. Her voice echoed in the room.

"Come quickly!"

Miriam rose and went toward the back door. There was a note of excitement in Alexandru's voice that piqued her curiosity. What was going on?

"Look!" Alexandru said, his usually placid face alive and glowing. "Look what Brother Pavel has given us!"

Miriam's eyes widened as she looked at the object in Alexandru's strong fingers. The clothbound book was black—could it be?

"What is it?" The question came out in a whisper as Miriam advanced slowly, her eyes fixed on the book.

"A Bible! Pavel gave us a Bible!" Alexandru said with emotion.

Miriam looked fully into their friend's face. Her eyes widened. She looked at the book again.

"A Bible! For us?" Her voice barely worked.

"Yes, for you," Pavel replied joyfully.

Miriam reached out and gently stroked the cover of the Bible. *Biblia.* It was not just the New Testament, for it did not say *Novea Zavet* on the cover. It said *Biblia.* It was the entire Bible!

"It is a gift for you," Pavel said. "For your very own."

"But I don't understand," Miriam said in amazement. "How is it possible that we should get a Bible? I mean, who … how … where did it come from?"

"It came from God," Pavel said with a smile. "This book is a gift from God to you."

"I know!" Miriam almost babbled. "I know that, but how did it get here?"

Alexandru handed the Bible to his wife. Miriam reverently opened the pages. She found the Psalms. She paged some more. The pages were of good quality and the binding well-done. It was a good Bible!

"But is it really for us?" she questioned again, closing the Bible and hugging it against her chest. "For us to keep?"

Pavel nodded. "Yes, for you. God used some of His children to provide this gift for you."

Miriam knew she would never find out just how the Bible had found its way to their home, but her mind traveled to many who must have worked hard and perhaps suffered in order for them to have this blessed gift.

"We must pray for all the people who were willing to sacrifice in order for us to have this gift. O Lord, bless them richly. Send your Spirit to bless them with your presence.

"Today, God has blessed our home." Miriam turned with joy to her husband. "We are supremely blessed to see this day." Almost dancing, she turned back to their visitor. "Oh, blessed are you, our friend and brother. You have brought this precious gift to us." Tears began coursing down her cheeks as she impulsively lifted the Bible up to her lips and kissed it with reverence.

"I don't need to copy it anymore!" Miriam suddenly remembered what she had been doing. "I don't need to copy it anymore!" She flexed the fingers on her free hand. "We have our own copy! We can read it any time we want!"

She saw Alexandru's eyes flit to the high fence that separated their yard from the neighbor's. She understood. She would have to lower her voice.

Yes, there was cause for rejoicing, but Miriam was also keenly aware that this Bible could be confiscated. She knew all about the persecution and danger involved in owning a Bible. She would have to control herself, but nothing could quench the joy that surged up in her heart. Nothing! She wanted to shout, sing, and give vent to her feelings. A Bible! They had received a Bible! She wanted to run and tell all her neighbors and the people in the church.

Reason prevailed, or at least restraint, but no matter what she was allowed to do, one thing was for sure, she was shouting inside!

Before their friend left, the three bowed their heads in prayer. First of all they thanked God for His goodness in sending His written Word to them. They thanked Him for the people who were involved in bringing Bibles to their country and for the people who initially had the vision to help the oppressed people who were longing for Bibles of their own.

Oh, the praise that Miriam sent winging upward as she poured out her feelings to her Saviour! She struggled to find words to express her feelings, resorting sometimes to silent tears, and other times to bubbling praise.

Long after Pavel had left, Miriam and Alexandru sat inside their house, turning the pages, reading passages, and marveling at the miracle they held in their hands.

"I will give my copy of the Gospel of John to someone else," Miriam said as she cleared the table for their simple supper. "I know someone else will be glad for the first three chapters they won't have to copy." Then, looking at her husband, she said soberly, "And if someone wants to borrow the Bible, should we let them?"

"What do you think?" Alexandru asked.

Miriam thought back to the long time of waiting she had gone through before she could even borrow the handwritten copy of the Gospel of John. She remembered with what joy she had finally gotten her turn to borrow the notebook and how excited she was when she was copying the blessed words.

"Yes," she nodded. "I know how the others feel. But could we … would it be all right for us to keep it at least for a little while? Maybe until we have read all the way through the New Testament?"

Alexandru nodded. "You know that won't take very long. We can begin tonight."

Looking thoughtfully at the Bible, Miriam said wistfully, "I am praying that one day everyone who wants a Bible can have one. Wouldn't that be wonderful, Alexandru, to have a Bible for every household! That is riches hard to comprehend!" Miriam had to smile at the very thought.

Once more, the couple bowed their heads and began to pray, the precious book held lovingly between them.

The above story was reenacted, with some variation, thousands of times in different places as the Bibles reached their destinations. The recipients did not even receive the Scriptures from the hand of a Bible courier. More often, the pastors would tell the members that gifts were available in a certain place. Everyone knew what that meant, and there would be a rush for the Bibles, New Testaments, or Gospels. Rarely did anyone know how the Bibles got there. There was no one to thank for all the work and efforts of bringing the written Word to the people.

That is, there was no one to thank but God. As the prayers of the grateful believers ascended to the throne of God, as the heartfelt cries of joy wafted upwards like incense, the mission of those touched and moved by God to be involved in Bible smuggling was realized. Their heart's desire was for God to receive glory and for men and women to be changed by the blessed book, the Holy Bible.

About the Author

Harvey Yoder and his wife Karen live in the beautiful mountains of western North Carolina. They have five children, all of whom are married, as well as eight grandchildren. A teacher for many years, Harvey is now a licensed real estate agent in addition to being a prolific writer. He has traveled extensively while gathering materials for his many books, most of which have been published by Christian Aid Ministries. Harvey finds it especially fulfilling to write the inspiring accounts of faithful believers whose stories would otherwise remain unknown. His greatest desire in writing is that his readers will not merely be entertained by the stories, but rather be motivated to seek God with all their hearts.

Harvey enjoys hearing from readers and can be contacted by e-mail at harveYoder@juno.com or written in care of Christian Aid Ministries, P.O. Box 360, Berlin, Ohio, 44610.

Christian Aid Ministries

Christian Aid Ministries (CAM) was founded in 1981 as a nonprofit, tax-exempt, 501(c)(3) organization. Our primary purpose is to provide a trustworthy, efficient channel for Amish, Mennonite, and other conservative Anabaptist groups and individuals to minister to physical and spiritual needs around the world.

Annually, CAM distributes approximately fifteen million pounds of food, clothing, medicines, seeds, Bibles, Bible story books, and other Christian literature. Most of the aid goes to needy children, orphans, and Christian families. The main purposes of giving material aid are to help and encourage God's people and to bring the Gospel to a lost and dying world.

CAM's home office is in Berlin, Ohio. In Ephrata, Pennsylvania, CAM has a 55,000 square feet distribution center where food parcels are packed and other relief shipments organized. Next to the distribution center is our meat canning facility. CAM is also associated with seven clothing centers—located in Indiana, Iowa, Illinois, Maryland, Pennsylvania, West Virginia, and Ontario, Canada—where clothing, footwear, comforters, and fabric are received, sorted, and prepared for shipment overseas.

CAM has staff, bases, and distribution networks in Romania, Moldova, Ukraine, Haiti, Nicaragua, Liberia, and Israel. Through our International Crisis (IC) program we also help victims of famine, war, and natural disasters throughout the world. In the USA, volunteers organized under our Disaster Response Services (DRS) program help rebuild in low-income communities devastated by natural disasters such as floods, tornados, and hurricanes. We operate medical clinics in Haiti and Nicaragua.

CAM is controlled by a ten-member board of directors and operated by a five-member executive committee. The organizational structure includes an audit review committee, executive council, ministerial committee, several support committees, and department managers.

CAM is largely a volunteer organization aside from management, supervisory personnel, and bookkeeping operations. Each year, volunteers at our warehouses, field bases, and on Disaster Response Services and International Crisis projects donate more than 200,000 hours.

CAM issues an annual, audited financial statement to its entire mailing list (statements are also available upon request). Fundraising and non-aid administrative expenses are kept as low as possible. Usually these expenses are about one percent of income, which includes cash and donated items in kind.

CAM's ultimate goal is to glorify God and enlarge His kingdom. ". . .whatsoever ye do, do all to the glory of God." (1 Corinthians 10:31)

For more information or to sign up for CAM's monthly newsletter, please write or call:

Christian Aid Ministries
P.O. Box 360
Berlin, OH 44610
Phone: 330.893.2428
Fax: 330.893.2305

Glossary

Alexandru	*(ah lehk SAHN droo)*	Alexander
Alexei	*(Ah lyek SYAY)*	
Ana	*(AH nah)*	Anna
Bârsan	*(BOOHR suhn)*	
Betuel	*(Bet oo ee YEHL)*	
Biblia	*(BEE blee yah)*	Bible
Codrean	*(KOH dreh ahn)*	
Corni	*(KOHR nee)*	
Constanţa	*(kohn STAHN tsah)*	
		city in southeastern Romania
Chilişeni	*(kee lee SHEHN)*	
Chişinau	*(KISH ee noh)*	
Cernauţi	*(chehr nah OOTS)*	city in Ukraine
Daniela	*(dah nee YEH lah)*	Danielle
Daniel	*(dah nee YEHL)*	Daniel
Dorel	*(doh REHL)*	
Dacia	*(DAH chyah)*	a Romanian-made car
Emil Andrieş	*(ay MEEL AHN dree ehsh)*	
Eugen	*(ay oo JEHN)*	Eugene
Gabriel	*(GAH bree ehl)*	
Gheorghe	*(GYOHR geh)*	George
Gigi	*(JEE jee)*	
Gherla	*(GEHR lah)*	city in Romania
Iaşi	*(Yahsh)*	city in Romania
Ilie	*(EE lee eh)*	Elijah
Iosif	*(YOH seef)*	Joseph

Ivan	*(ee VAHN)*	John
Lila	*(LEE lah)*	
Lidia	*(LEE dee yah)*	Lydia
Lucia	*(LOO chyah)*	
Luci	*(LOO chee)*	
Marcu	*(MAHR koo)*	Mark
Marian	*(mah ree AHN)*	
Mihai	*(mee HI)*	Michael
Miriam	*(MEHR ee yahm)*	
Minsk	*(MEENSK)*	city in Belarus
Monica	*(moh NEE kah)*	
Natasha	*(nah TAH shah)*	
Nicolae	*(nee koh LAH eh)*	
Novea Zavet	*(NOH vee ah Zah VET)*	
Pace	*(PAH cheh)*	"peace," used as a greeting among the Romanian evangelical believers
Pasha	*(PAH shuh)*	
Pavel	*(PAH vehl)*	Paul
Romică	*(roh MEE kah)*	
Sara	*(SAH rah)*	
Silviu	*(SEEL veeoo)*	
Slavic	*(SLAH veek)*	
Sibiu	*(see BEE oo)*	city in Romania
Suceava	*(soo CHYAH vah)*	city in northeastern Romania
Tata	*(TAH tah)*	Daddy
Teofil	*(TEH oh feel)*	
Valentin	*(vah len TEEN)*	
Victor	*(veek TOHR)*	
Yulia	*(YOO lee ah)*	
Yuri	*(YOOH ree)*	
Zaharia	*(Zah ah REE yah)*	Zacharia

Additional Books from

Christian Aid Ministries

God Knows My Size! / *by Harvey Yoder*
Raised in communist Romania, Silvia Tarniceriu struggled to believe in God. But His direct answer to her earnest prayer convinced Silvia that God is real, and that He knows all about her. This book is excellent for family reading time.
251 pages $10.99

They Would Not Be Silent / *by Harvey Yoder*
In this book, each of the stories about Christians under communism is unique, yet one mutual thread runs throughout—they would not be silent concerning their devotion to the Lord Jesus.
231 pages $10.99

They Would Not Be Moved / *by Harvey Yoder*
A sequel to *They Would Not Be Silent,* this book contains more true stories about Christians who did not lose courage under the cruel hand of communism. It is our prayer that the moving stories will encourage you and help you to be stronger in your faith in the Lord Jesus Christ and more thankful for the freedoms we enjoy in our country.
208 pages $10.99

Elena—Strengthened Through Trials / *by Harvey Yoder*
Born into a poor Christian family in communist Romania, after harsh treatment at a state boarding school and harassment from

authorities for helping in secret Bible distribution, Elena finally decides to flee her home country. Will she make it? A true story.

240 pages $10.99

Where Little Ones Cry / *by Harvey Yoder*

This is a story about war in Liberia. In the midst of the terror that war brings are the little children. Their stories, a few of which are captured in this book, are not of typical, carefree children. Some of these true accounts have happy endings, but sad trails lead them there. The purpose of this book is not to entertain, but to help you appreciate our blessed country more and create awareness of the pain and spiritual darkness that abound in much of Africa.

168 pages plus 16-page picture section $10.99

Wang Ping's Sacrifice / *by Harvey Yoder*

The true stories in this book vividly portray the house church in China and the individuals at its heart. Read how the church—strong, flourishing, and faithful in spite of persecution—is made up of real people with real battles. Witness their heartaches and triumphs, and find your own faith strengthened and refreshed.

191 pages $10.99

A Small Price to Pay / *by Harvey Yoder*

Living in the Soviet Union under cruel, atheistic communism and growing up during World War II, young Mikhail Khorev saw much suffering and death. Often homeless and near starvation, he struggled to believe in God's love. This inspiring story of how Mikhail grew to be a man of God, willing to suffer prison for the God who loved him, will move you to tears and strengthen your faith. You, too, will come to realize that everything we can give to the Christ who saves us is still . . . A Small Price to Pay.

247 pages $11.99

Tears of the Rain
by Ruth Ann Stelfox
The moving story of a missionary family struggling to help some of the poorest people in the world—the men, women, and children of war-torn Liberia. Vividly descriptive and poignantly honest, this story will have you laughing on one page and crying on the next.

479 pages $13.99

Tsunami!—*from a few that survived* / *by Harvey Yoder*
Just like that, one of the greatest natural disasters in modern history approached the city of Banda Aceh, Indonesia. For most people, the cries of "Water!" reached them too late. But some survived to tell the story.

As you read the accounts in this book, you will experience, in a small degree, a few of the horrors that the people of Banda Aceh faced. Some tell their stories with sorrow and heartbreak, others with joy and hope.

168 pages $11.99

A Greater Call / *by Harvey Yoder*
Born into a poor family in famine-racked China, young Wei was left to die. But God had a different plan. Wei would one day answer a greater call. The cost would be enormous, but to Wei and other Chinese Christians, Jesus Christ was worth any sacrifice.

195 pages $11.99

Angels in the Night / *by Pablo Yoder*
Pablo's family had endured more than a dozen robberies during their first two years as missionaries in Nicaragua. But God had called them to Waslala, and they had faith that He would protect them.

In spite of the poverty and violence that surrounded them, a fledgling church was emerging, and a light, small at first but growing steadily, was piercing the darkness.

Angels in the Night continues the story begun in *Angels Over Waslala*, chronicling the trials and joys of this missionary family.

356 pages $12.99

In Search of Home / *by Harvey Yoder*

If Zumrat accepted the Christian God, her family would disown her, her husband would despise her, and she might even be killed. Still . . . what if this Christian God could give her the peace she longed for so much? The true story of a Muslim family's miraculous conversion, followed by persecution and a grueling journey in search of a place to call home.

240 pages $11.99

The Happening / *by Harvey Yoder*

The shootings at the Nickel Mines Amish schoolhouse shocked the nation and the world. This is the heartrending story of the young victims, their families, and the community as they struggled to come to grips with this tragedy. How could they find peace and forgive the man who had caused their grief? The true details of *The Happening* are woven into a story told through the eyes and heart of one young survivor.

173 pages $11.99

HeartBridge / *by Johnny Miller*

The Nathaniel Christian Orphanage in Romania opened its doors in 1992 as a home for hurting children. By the time Johnny and Ruth Miller arrived to be tata and mama, the orphanage housed 53 precious children. These are the touching—and sometimes heart-wrenching—stories of the Millers' first year in Romania.

272 pages $12.99

The Long Road Home / *Pablo Yoder*

To young Pablo, moving to Costa Rica was one big adventure. But his innocent adventures took a darker turn down a lonely and increasingly wicked path. Inside, a Voice was calling, but Pablo, hungry for excitement, wasn't ready to listen. Would his parents' prayers and the gentle promptings of the Spirit bring him back "home"? Photos and sketches throughout the book.

456 pages $12.99

Labors of Love

Full of photos, memories, and stories, this hardcover keepsake book is a tribute to the volunteers who served on CAM's Disaster Response Services and International Crisis projects from 2002-2006. Read about:

• God's people responding to Hurricane Katrina
• Work among the poor in the mountains of Pakistan
• Volunteers praying for a despairing hurricane victim
• God miraculously providing a boat for a stranded man

• and much more!

Hardcover. Full-color photos. 9" x 11½"
160 pages. $19.99 or 2 for $30

Miss Nancy / *Harvey Yoder*

This is the inspiring and fascinating story of God's work in the life of an Amish missionary to Belize. Miss Nancy Coblentz is known and loved by thousands, from street waifs to statesmen, from paupers to a prime minister. Whether in drudgery, danger, or success, her dauntless faith and devotion have inspired and challenged countless people. You will be amazed at the God who uses ordinary people to produce extraordinary results.

273 pages $11.99

A Heart to Belong / *by Johnny Miller*

A Heart to Belong (sequel to HeartBridge) continues the story of God's sustaining grace as the Millers love and guide the children of the Nathaniel Christian Orphanage in Romania.

302 pages $12.99

A Life Redeemed / *by Harvey Yoder*

The inspiring story of Ludlow Walker's journey from his childhood in Jamacia to his current calling as a minister of the Gospel. An unforgettable story of God's redeeming grace and transforming power.

232 pages $11.99

Steps to Salvation

The Bible says that we all have "sinned and come short of the glory of God" (Romans 3:23). We sin because we give heed to our sinful nature inherited from Adam's sin in the Garden of Eden, and our sin separates us from God.

God provided the way back to Himself by His only Son, Jesus Christ, who became the spotless Lamb "slain from the foundation of the world." "For God so loved the world that he gave his only begotten Son, that whosoever believeth in him should not perish, but have everlasting life" (John 3:16).

To be reconciled to God and experience life rather than death, and heaven rather than hell (Deuteronomy 30:19), we must repent and believe in the Son of God, the Lord Jesus Christ (Romans 6:32; 6:16).

When we sincerely repent of our sins (Acts 2:38; 3:19; 17:30) and by faith receive Jesus Christ as our Saviour and Lord, God saves us by His grace and we are born again. "That if thou shalt confess with thy mouth the Lord Jesus, and shalt believe in thine heart that God hath raised him from the dead, thou shalt be saved" (Romans 10:9). "For by grace are ye saved through faith; and that not of yourselves: it is the gift of God" (Ephesians 2:8).

When we become born again in Jesus Christ, we become new creatures (2 Corinthians 5:17). We do not continue in sin (1 John 3:9), but give testimony of our new life in Jesus

Christ by baptism and obedience to Him. "He that hath my commandments, and keepeth them, he it is that loveth me: and he that loveth me shall be loved of my Father, and I will love him, and will manifest myself to him" (John 14:21).

To grow spiritually, we need to meditate on God's Word and commune with God in prayer. Fellowship with a faithful group of believers is also important to strengthen and maintain our Christian walk (1 John 1:7).